A USER-FRIENDLY UNIVERSE?

SPIRITUAL SPEECHES in an ACADEMIC CONTEXT

CLIFFORD CHALMERS CAIN

WestBow Press
A DIVISION OF THOMAS NELSON & ZONDERVAN

Copyright © 2016 Clifford Chalmers Cain.

All rights reserved. No part of this book may be used or reproduced by any means, graphic, electronic, or mechanical, including photocopying, recording, taping or by any information storage retrieval system without the written permission of the author except in the case of brief quotations embodied in critical articles and reviews.

New Revised Standard Version Bible, copyright © 1989, Division of Christian Education of the National Council of the Churches of Christ in the United States of America. Used by permission. All rights reserved.

This book is a work of non-fiction. Unless otherwise noted, the author and the publisher make no explicit guarantees as to the accuracy of the information contained in this book and in some cases, names of people and places have been altered to protect their privacy.

WestBow Press books may be ordered through booksellers or by contacting:

WestBow Press
A Division of Thomas Nelson & Zondervan
1663 Liberty Drive
Bloomington, IN 47403
www.westbowpress.com
1 (866) 928-1240

Because of the dynamic nature of the Internet, any web addresses or links contained in this book may have changed since publication and may no longer be valid. The views expressed in this work are solely those of the author and do not necessarily reflect the views of the publisher, and the publisher hereby disclaims any responsibility for them.

Any people depicted in stock imagery provided by Thinkstock are models, and such images are being used for illustrative purposes only. Certain stock imagery © Thinkstock.

ISBN: 978-1-5127-3559-8 (sc)
ISBN: 978-1-5127-3558-1 (e)

Library of Congress Control Number: 2016909690

Print information available on the last page.

WestBow Press rev. date: 6/23/2016

Dedicated to Jim and Sharon Harrod, whose generosity established an endowed professorship and whose kindness enriches our friendship.

And in memory and honor of Ethel Virginia Bokelman Cain, a giving, loving, and patient mother, who nurtured me in the Christian faith.

Table of Contents

Foreword ix
Preface xiii
Acknowledgments xv
A User-friendly Universe? 1
A God on the Move 7
Descending Into Hell 12
Apollo or Dionysus? 18
Take Courage! 24
Ahadun and the Three Golden Calves 30
Masks 36
Why Are *We* Blessed? 43
The Word Became *Flesh*! 48
999 Patrons 53
The Essence of Christianity 58
Christ and Culture 63
What Is Faith? 69
Fools, for Christ's Sake! 74
Guilty 80
Hidalgo 85
Buried for Lack of Appreciation 91
The Spring of Hope 97
Tariki-Jiriki 104
Keeping Sabbath throughout Our Lives 111
The Erratic Behavior of Lunatics 116

3-D Glasses 125
Somewhere Under the Rainbow 131
The Sweet Sorrow of Departure 135
About the Author 141

Foreword

We expect a lot from our colleges and universities. We always have. From the time of the first Colonial Colleges right through to today's Research Universities, we have tasked our institutions of higher learning to transfer our values to the next generation. Colleges and universities are to inform our children's intellects and train their hands for the good of the Republic. And from the beginning, we have also expected post-secondary schools to form the hearts of their inhabitants. Despite growing and contrary pressures from industry, legislatures, and other interest groups, college remains a place and a time for spiritual formation.

Spirits are still being shaped and strengthened at colleges and universities. Today more than ever, those who direct this dimension of higher education's mission recognize the breadth and depth of their objective. Witness the renewed emphasis on service. Offices of academic and student affairs across the country now include community service requirements among their students' extra-curricular activities. At the university where I teach, 700 freshmen recently spent a day doing volunteer community service with civic, social service, and commercial partners in our city. My *alma mater* did not have me do that when I was a freshman. It does now. Colleges and universities are more committed than ever to increasing students' cross-cultural understanding. Study abroad is becoming the norm, and while the cost of such study still keeps many from receiving its benefits, most students now receive research-based and practical instruction about other cultures in required *general education* courses. Another example comes to mind, one that is unfortunately more a reaction to tragic incidents than the result of intentional commitment. Members of fraternities and sororities on campuses across the country are increasingly participating in mandatory training on sexual assault awareness. Those mandatory training sessions are spiritual formation, as are spring break mission trips and cultural diversity classes.

These and other initiatives in higher education today are purposeful forays into the field of spiritual formation, a field that in earlier times was largely occupied by practices and practitioners of the dominant faith traditions. To consider training sessions and mission trips spiritual formation is certainly to broaden the field beyond what trustees of the Colonial Colleges envisioned. But should we not consider it a broadening by addition? When we *add* cultural diversity classes to required freshman Bible surveys and required chapel attendance, doesn't spiritual formation become richer, stronger, more far-reaching?

A User-friendly Universe? seeks to push the limits of spiritual formation in a similar way. It offers spiritual edification by extending it, by addressing the head as well as the heart. These chapters are meditations of a faithful academic intended to edify faithful folks in the academy, but also to stretch their thinking. Students, professors, administrators, and staff members who are serious about spiritual growth will find them engaging. So will others who are not directly or still connected with the academy.

Cliff Cain reads the Christian scriptures closely, and in light of the longer arc of the Christian tradition. He's also a perceptive reader of the Western scientific tradition, as his previous books on environmental theology and his recent book on the relationship between science and religion clearly indicate. He's an experienced border-ranger, a veteran of long years exploring (patrolling? extending?) the frontiers between science and religion, faith and reason. But here, I'll go ahead and say it, he reveals his pastor's heart in this book. These meditations are as warm as they are thought-provoking. Our guide is trustworthy, so our minds and our souls can be fortified. With him, let's extend the field of spiritual formation for the good of the Kingdom.

The Rev. Fr. Marshall Crossnoe, Ph.D.
Professor of History, Lincoln University
Jefferson City, Missouri
Vicar of St. Alban's Episcopal Church
Fulton, Missouri
Vicar of St. Mark's Episcopal Church
Portland, Missouri

Preface

A full and dynamic Christian faith involves the mind as well as the heart, the intellect as well as the spirit, reason as well as emotion. What we think and what we feel contribute to how we nurture our lives as Christians and walk our Christian journey. An emotional impact must be fortified by intellectual simulation, and rational discourse must be enriched by spiritual motivation. Indeed, Jesus at one point admonishes us to love God with all our heart, soul, strength, and mind (Luke 10:27a; Matthew 22:37; cf. Deuteronomy 6:5), as well as to love other people as we love ourselves (Luke 10:27b; Matthew 22:39; cf. Leviticus 19:18).

The religious presentations or faith talks or "spiritual speeches" in this volume were given in collegiate academic contexts and were intended to stimulate mental response and provide spiritual edification. They focus on themes and issues that are relevant to the cycles of the academic year, the seasons of the Christian calendar, and the rhythms of the Christian life. Thus, they provide reflections on the beginning of the school year, spiritual discipline and celebration, Thanksgiving, Christmas, Epiphany, April Fools' Day, Easter, and graduation, as well as on theological topics such as God's omnipresence, spiritual transformation, incarnational theology, self-worth, the relationship of Christianity and culture, Christian virtues, environmental concerns, the Kingdom of God, and Christian hope.

The prospect of having these meditations available to a wider public is exciting. And it is hoped that they might nourish the spirit and uplift the mind of the reader.

> Clifford Chalmers Cain
> Westminster College
> Fulton, Missouri

Acknowledgments

The author would like to thank the Rev. Jon Lowell Lineback and Mr. Tim Fitch of WestBow Press, a division of Thomas Nelson and Zondervan Publishers, for their encouragement and guidance; former work-study students and now Westminster College *alumni*, Saifon Liangpansakul and Noah Lennon, for their help with the manuscript; friend and colleague in teaching and in ministry, the Rev. Fr. Marshall Crossnoe, Ph.D., Professor of History at Lincoln University in Jefferson City, Missouri, and Vicar of St. Alban's Episcopal Church in Fulton, Missouri, and Vicar of St. Mark's Episcopal Church in Portland, Missouri, for writing his gracious and generous Foreword; Westminster College President and person of faith and of vision, Dr. Benjamin Ola. Akande, for his comments in the midst of a busy schedule while beginning his new position; Dr. Janice Thompson, Associate Professor of Theology and Chairperson of the Department of Theology at King's College in Wilkes-Barre, Pennsylvania, for her reflections; long-time friend and former Executive Director of the Indiana Office for Campus Ministries, the Rev. Erwin Bode, for reading and reacting to the manuscript; Milan Doles, Westminster College '16, for the author's photo; and finally, not only the persons who invited me to write and make these presentations but also the individuals who chose to come listen to them and then to converse with me about them.

Appreciation is also expressed to the following for permission to quote from their materials:

New Revised Standard Version Bible © 1989 Division of Christian Education of the National Council of the Churches of Christ in the United States of America. Used by permission. All rights reserved.

John E. Carroll *et al*. ***The Greening of Faith***, pp. 219-220. © 1997 The Trustees of the University of New Hampshire. University Press of New England, Hanover, New Hampshire. Reprinted with permission of University Press of New England.

Over the Rainbow (from "The Wizard of Oz"). Music by Harold Arlen. Lyrics by E.Y. Harburg. © 1938 (Renewed) Metro-Goldwyn-Mayer Inc. © 1939 (Renewed) EMI Feist Catalog Inc. All Rights Controlled and Administered by EMI Feist Catalog Inc. (Publishing) and Alfred Music (Print). All Rights Reserved.

If You Leave Me Now. Words and Music by Peter Cetera. Copyright © 1976 by Universal Music – MGB Songs and Spirit Catalogue Holdings, S.a.r.l. Copyright Renewed. All Rights for Spirit Catalogue Holdings, S.a.r.l. in the United States, U.K. and Canada. Administered by Spirit Two Music, Inc. All Rights for Spirit Catalogue Holdings, S.a.r.l. for the rest of the world Administered by Spirit Service Holdings, S.a.r.l. International Copyright Secured. All Rights Reserved. *Reprinted by Permission of Hal Leonard Corporation.*

A User-friendly Universe?

Computers, laptops, notebooks, ipads, and smart phones are all commonplace today. We use them without thinking about it. In fact, we can hardly imagine a time when we didn't have them. They're as prevalent as air, and as seemingly necessary as breathing.

Yet I can remember both a time when there were no computers and the day when I got my first computer: The large box with the Leading Edge computer arrived unceremoniously—it was just "there" when I arrived home from work. I opened it, and alas, there was this strange concoction of keyboard, screen, disk drives, and a labyrinth of coiled, snake-like electrical cords and hook-ups, and a voluminous instruction book perched blatantly on top of this mountain of materials. This sight posed an intimidating challenge: Would I be able to set-up this "state of the art" collection of metal and plastic and rubber and glass?

As I removed the contents from the box—fearing that, like Pandora, I was releasing all forms of evil into the world—I noticed the big block letters: They were stamped prominently on the cover of the instruction book and on the inside of the container—"THIS COMPUTER IS USER-FRIENDLY." What appeared to be formidable, even hostile, was in actuality not ominous at all. In fact, it was designed to be positive—"friendly"—in relationship to me.

Drawn ahead, then, by a mixture of relief and new-found confidence, I plunged into the wonderful world of computers!

The eighteenth century German writer, Gotthold Lessing, once remarked that if he could ask the Sphinx—that monumental, architectural wonder outside Cairo, Egypt, with a lion's body and a human's head—only one question, it would be this: "Is the universe friendly, or not?"

There is much that suggests that the *cosmos* is *un*friendly: Our newspapers, televisions, and iphones stream to us and scream at us disturbing incidents and events of pain, misfortune, injustice, calamity, and unmitigated evil. The world seems filled with hunger, war, death, poverty, deprivation, and nastiness.

According to theologian J. Edward Barrett in his book, *Faith in Focus*, all religions ask three basic questions:

(1) What kind of world do I live in?
(2) How am I meant to live in this world?
(3) Where can I find the strength to live that way?

In other words, beyond all our everyday thoughts and experiences, religion wants to know about the great, overarching themes, the "big picture": Is the world friendly or unfriendly? How should human life respond to this world? And, is there some source of help for making that response?

The answers of a particular religion make-up something like a painting—with a landscape in the background, a person in the foreground, and some symbol for a source of courage and strength. The "landscape" provides a general view of what the world is like (according to that religion). The "person in the foreground" provides a model for living appropriately in that kind of world. And the "symbol" provides a guide to where help can be found to live that kind of life.

Of course, the different religions of the world paint different pictures. And, as a Christian, I have faith/trust that the picture painted by Christianity is accurate. To be religious, in my view, is to trust in, and be committed to, a particular picture—that is, to hope that that picture is true, and to have faith in it.

The meaning of the Christian faith for me is that the Christian picture proclaims (1) that the world is fundamentally good, as Genesis 1:31 proclaims; (2) that love is the meaning of life, as I John 4:7 and Ephesians 1:5 hold; and (3) that the Holy Spirit is the source of "grace to help in time of need," as Hebrews 4:16 says.

Of course, there are many details, shades of meaning, and subtleties which my summary omits. But, to me, this is the essential outline of the Christian picture, the Gospel (or "Good News"). Because "God is love" (I John 4:8, 16), the landscape is good; because God is love, it makes sense to live and love as Jesus lived and loved (I John 4:11; Ephesians 5:1-2); and because God is love, it is possible to grow "strong in the grace that is in Christ" (II Timothy 2:1). In other words, the universe is "user-friendly."

The Bible certainly pictures God as "Creator," "Lord," and "Judge." These titles and images hold a strong power for me. But the picture of God in the Bible as "Father" has the greatest personal impact: Jesus himself told us to call God "Abba," and to pray to God as "Abba"—an intimate, Aramaic reference to family life. "Father" is perhaps too formal a translation; nowadays, most commentators liken Abba to "Daddy."

The picture of God as "Abba"—as 'Daddy'—suggests that at the heart of the universe, in the depths of what Einstein called "mystery," there is a divine reality which is related to us personally, which cares about us, which forgives us, and which loves us so much that God is willing to suffer with us and sacrifice for us, not only 2000 years ago in the figure of Jesus especially, but yesterday, today, and tomorrow.

In Greek mythology, the god Prometheus had compassion on humankind, for men and women did not possess fire. Without fire, life was a cheerless and comfortless existence. So Prometheus took fire from heaven and gave it as a gift to the world. Zeus, the king of the gods, came "unglued" with anger that humans had received this gift of fire, and had received it at the hands of such a "Benedict Arnold" as Prometheus. So Zeus took Prometheus and chained him to a rock in the middle of the Adriatic Sea, where he was tortured with the heat and thirst of the day, and the cold of the night. And, adding insult to injury, Zeus arranged for a vulture to tear out Prometheus' liver, which always grew back again, only to have it torn out once more.

According to Greek legend, that is what happened to the god who dared to care about the plight of human beings and tried to help them. The picture here is of gods who are petty, jealous, vengeful, and grudging; and the last thing that gods are willing to do is come to the assistance of those humans who need it.

Not so with the God of the Bible, the Father ("Abba"—'Daddy') of the Christian faith, and the deity whose love frames the Christian picture: Deuteronomy 26 (cf. Exodus 3:7-10) tells of a God who heard the cries of the Israelites bound in Egyptian slavery and forced to erect granaries and storehouses in the Goshen area of Egypt. And not only did this God hear those cries, God responded to them, delivering the Israelites "out of Egypt with a mighty hand and an outstretched arm" (vs. 8).

This understanding of God, a God known as "Daddy," who cares enough to liberate humans from whatever binds them, *literally* makes all the difference in the world. And so, the universe has operating within it the presence and activity of a Reality and a Power for good whom we Christians name as "God." Thus, we need not huddle in fear and trembling at the prospect of hostile gods nor at the experience of a world that is less than as it was originally created by God, and still remains less than it will finally be. For we are encouraged by a Father's love.

The natural scientist, Loren Eiseley, was in a seaside town for vacation. Plagued by insomnia, he spent the early morning hours walking the beach. Each day at sunrise, he found some of the townspeople combing the sand for starfish, which had washed ashore during the night, in order to kill them for commercial purposes. Eiseley thought this to be a sign, however small, of all the ways in which the world is hostile to life.

A User-friendly Universe?

One morning, however, Eiseley got up unusually early, and discovered a solitary figure on the beach. This person, too, was gathering starfish, but each time she found one alive, she would pick it up and throw it as far as she could beyond the breaking surf. As days went by, Eiseley found this person embarking on this mission of mercy each morning, seven days a week, no matter what the weather.

Eiseley called this person the "star thrower." The harm and hostility were symbolically contradicted by one individual who reached down to save the helpless. Eiseley wondered if there is a star-thrower at work in the universe, a God who works to redeem a world that was created "good," but now is less than this God prefers. A "star-thrower God," he concluded, must be one whose nature is compassion, love, and mercy.

In the history of Israel and in the person and work of Jesus of Nazareth, we see present and reflected the mercy, love, and compassion of our star-thrower Father. In the story of Israel, we see a God who toils for liberation, justice, and social responsibility. In the person of Jesus, we come face-to-face with a God who loves, suffers, forgives, and redeems.

The Christian faith means to me that the universe is user-friendly. God sacrifices God's own well-being for us (because God loves us), God conquers our sin by absorbing its hurt (because God is gracious), and God shows us how to live appropriately and meaningfully in such a world (because God cares about us). When you and I love God and love one another, we fulfill our destiny and become what God created us to be (as Deuteronomy 19, Mark 12, John 13, and Matthew 22 all testify).

So, the meaning of the Christian faith for me is captured in a painting, a painting which answers the three most basic questions of religion:

> Is the world friendly or unfriendly?
> How should we respond to this world?
> Is there some source of help for making that response?

In the background, the painting has a landscape or view of what the world is like—and it is pictured as good. The painting has a person or model of living in the foreground—and the love of Jesus is pictured as the way to live. The painting has a symbol which points to where help can be found to live that life—and the Holy Spirit is pictured as the source of grace. And finally, God is pictured as framing the whole painting with God's love.

In the name of the Father, the Son, and the Holy Spirit, I proclaim to you that the universe is user-friendly.*

Scripture for reflection: Deuteronomy 26:5b-9; Matthew 6:9-15; Genesis 1:31; I John 4:7; Ephesians 1:5; Hebrews 4:16

*[Of course, the reality of God lies beyond gender, and referring to God as "Father" (male) maintains the typical way of divine reference in the Christian tradition. This is patriarchal and sexist, unless one acknowledges that God is neither male nor female, and that using male nouns and pronouns is no more theologically accurate than using female nouns and pronouns. And, given the painful experience of abuse by fathers that some children have unfortunately and regrettably endured, "father" may not elicit the positive qualities that are intended. However, designating God as "Parent" rather than as "Father" (or as "Mother")—though it avoids patriarchy and sexism—succumbs to a dilution and diminishing of the particularly and personally powerful love and care that are characteristic of the nature of God.]

A God on the Move

Four thousand years ago, that area of the world known as the Ancient Near East underwent tremendous social change: Mass migrations of people were one of the results. I can imagine that this situation must have looked much like students and their families heading-off to college each fall across the United States.

One such ancient emigrant was Abram (who would later become known as "Abraham")—son of Terah—whose family had already moved once before! Abraham trekked from what is modern-day Iraq to what is modern-day Israel: He moved first to Shechem, then he re-located to the east of Bethel. Following this, he continued his journey into the Negev Desert.

What's quite interesting about this trek is that every place to which Abraham went, he built an altar to God. He built an altar at Shechem, and he erected an altar at Bethel. It is safe to presume that this pattern continued, and that Abraham constructed an altar to God at his next location. Abraham was a guy on the move. And Abraham planned to worship God no matter where he was, no matter where he went.

You yourselves were participants in a migration of sorts: Several days ago, you packed up your stuff, crammed it into a family vehicle (or two!) and journeyed to this place. Upon arrival, you unloaded your "migration machines" and stuffed your belongings into a residence hall room which perhaps seemed much smaller than you remembered from campus tours or from summer registration or from last year if you are a returning student.

And here you are (for a four-year sojourn or for your remaining-years sojourn) at this College. You have been persons on the move.

Now Abraham was confident that God had *called* him to his movement: He believed that God had said to him, "Go from your country and your kindred and your father's house to the land that I will show you."

But Abraham surely had at least *some* apprehension as well. He had to leave familiar territory, he had to leave the old neighborhood, he had to depart from family and friends. He had to say "good by" to his mom and dad.

And now he was in an unfamiliar place, amidst "Canaanites"—new people he did not know. How would he get along? How would he "fit-in"? Would he be successful? Would it be a "fun place"?

Like Abraham, you, too, have come to unfamiliar territory. You have left behind the house you grew up in, the family you grew up with, the dog, the cat, and the place you knew your way around; you probably even left your own Walmart and your own McDonald's! You said "good by" to your friends, you have said "good by" to your mom and dad, perhaps even "good by" to your boyfriend or girlfriend.

Of course, God has *brought* you to this new place at this moment in time. God has led you—through whatever means, by whatever routes—to this College. But are you confident—as Abraham was—that God has, indeed, *called* you? Are you aware and trusting that God has spoken to *you* and said, "Go from your countryside and your kindred and your father's house to the piece of land which I will show you and there you will dwell with other persons of unknown identities, with strange-sounding designations such as "seniors, juniors, sophomores, and freshmen" and "faculty, staff, and administrators"?

You have been called to this place at this moment in time. But, as was the case also with Abraham, you have not left God behind. It's not as if God said, "I call you to go forth from your homeland to a new place I will show you," and then continued, 'Oh, yeah, by the way, I, God, will not be going with you!' No, Abraham ventured forth believing that God would be accompanying him and that God would be found every place Abraham went. That's why Abraham built those altars and called upon the name of God in each location.

Abraham was a person on the move. And God was a *God* on the move!

You, like Abraham, have ventured forth from your homeland to this new place. But do you believe—do you trust—that you have *not* left God behind? Do you believe that you will meet God every place you go? Do you have confidence that you will "bump into" God *here*?

The Israelites momentarily lost this belief when they were in exile from the land of Canaan. Psalm 137:1-6 points to this. They were lamenting their plight in Babylon, 700 miles away from Jerusalem. The Babylonians had conquered them, and dragged them off, "kicking and screaming" to an unknown place and unfamiliar territory.

So, "how could they sing the Lord's song in a foreign land?" How could they worship God in another country? Wasn't God the God of the land of Israel? Wasn't God the God who took up lodging in the Jerusalem Temple? Didn't persons make religious pilgrimages to that Temple in order to worship the God who dwelt there?

If God was entirely "there," then God surely could not be simultaneously "here." So, maybe they left God back in the land of Judah. Maybe God had perimeters to God's presence; maybe there were boundaries to God's location.

Of course, they would, with time, come to their theological senses, and realize that God was with them no matter where they were. Later they would realize that their lament was unnecessary.

You see, for people of faith, no place is completely "God-forsaken!" There is no place where God is not! Since we have confidence in this, that means that God has been waiting for you here. Our God is a God on the move!

Perhaps you have already sensed the presence of God in people who have welcomed you, shown you the ropes, helped you find your way around town, helped you negotiate the turbulent waters of class scheduling, and assisted you in meeting people. Perhaps you will discern the grace and compassion and encouragement of God—

> in the kindness shown by an R.A. when you're homesick or when your roommate is just downright "impossible;"

Perhaps you will discern the grace and compassion and encouragement of God—

> in the help provided by a staff member when that tuition or scholarship check has not arrived on time;

Perhaps you will discern the grace and compassion and encouragement of God—

> in a faculty member who tells you not to worry too much but to study hard and you'll be okay in her course.

God went with Abraham, just as God was already ahead of Abraham awaiting him in an unfamiliar place and in an unknown future. In the same way, God has come with you here *and* has awaited your arrival, since God was already here! You did not leave God at home nor did you bring God with you to a location where God has never been. Indeed, there will never be a place to which you could ever go where God will not be present.

The same thing is true for Jesus. In his concluding statement to his disciples in the Gospel of Matthew, Jesus commands them to be about the business of making disciples. And then he says, "Lo, I am with you to the end of the age." Or, as we might hear this today,

A User-friendly Universe?

"Hey, I will be present with you until the end of time." You left neither God nor Jesus back in your hometown. They are here. You will never go to a place nor be doing a single thing that is at distance from the presence of Jesus Christ.

Abraham built altars every place he went. I'm not sure each of you needs to build himself/herself an altar in your room (there's surely not enough space!). But your "altar" can be made of something other than stones: When you plan your schedules, plan to take advantage of every spiritual opportunity you can, in order to grow in your faith. There will be worship services available for you. There will be interfaith gatherings for you to attend. There will be volunteer opportunities for you to join, there will be Bible studies in which you can participate, there are local churches where you can go and be welcomed and plug-in to your specific Christian denomination.

So, build an altar to God with your activities, your growth in faith, your spiritual maturity. You're here at this College now! What will your altar look like?

I think that one of the most important aspects of our Christian faith is recognizing, celebrating, and remembering that our God is a God on the move. This means that throughout your life God will be present with you everywhere you go, wherever you find yourself—whether right now at this place, or other places you'll go at future times in your life. Wherever you are, whatever you are doing—you can always rely on God's grace, God's love, God's support, God's forgiveness, and God's encouragement.

You didn't leave God at home! So, build an "altar" here, and now, to God in order to enrich your religious pilgrimage. God has brought you here. So, grow now and prosper in the place which is your new home, a "land which God has shown you," and to which God has *called* you!

Scripture for reflection: Genesis 12:1-9; Psalm 137:1-6; Matthew 28:5-10, 16-20

Descending Into Hell

In *The Iliad* of Homer, Odysseus, King of Ithaca, leaves his wife and son to sail away with his army on a military adventure. His mission?: To rescue Helen of Troy. Ten years of war follow. Another ten years later after the end of the war, Odysseus and his friends have still not returned home, preferring instead to sail from island to island, engaging in a fantastic series of adventures fighting giants and contending with monsters, gods, and goddesses.

In fact, the god of the sea, Poseidon, has it "in" for Odysseus and places one challenge after another in his way. However, in good Greek heroic form, Odysseus overcomes every challenge. The tales of these adventures are called *The Odyssey*, which together with *The Iliad*, is one of the great stories of world literature.

Through it all, Odysseus' wife and son wait faithfully at home, with no word of husband and father. Why should Odysseus return home, with so many adventures awaiting him on the sea?

The answer comes in Book XI, when Odysseus sails to the very edge of the world and enters the dark regions of Hades, where he meets the shadowy souls of the dead. The Greeks believed that when we die, we enter a dark, non-descript world of the shades. In Hades, Odysseus meets all the great Greek heroes from the past. Now, in death, they are as nothing. The dead want only news from the other world, news of friends and family. Seeing the emptiness of the state of these departed spirits, Odysseus realizes what is important and unimportant in life. In today's terms, we might say that he had a flash of insight, a revelation from the Divine, a penetrating "learning experience."

In a symbolic death and rebirth, Odysseus emerges from Hades a different person. He immediately prepares to head for home, to rejoin his wife and son, seeing that this relationship is the most important thing in his life.

I'm sure that all of us have heard about, even perhaps known personally, individuals who—after a serious accident, during surgery, in a time of deep, contemplative prayer, through a Bible study, after a mountaintop experience—have had flashes of intuition and perception and turn-arounds similar to that of Odysseus. They went to "Hades," so to speak; or they descended into "hell." They came face-to-face with the way things are, an insight resulted, and they were transformed: They came away from the experience, changed people.

Think about your own life for a moment. Can you recall moments when a fresh idea, a penetrating insight, or a life-changing conclusion emerged? Maybe it was when you realized for the first time that all physical things die; or that the world is a violent place; or that things don't always turn out the way we would like; or that you would indeed be going to college; or that you would choose to come to this College; or that you were really, truly, deeply in love with someone. Maybe it was when you accepted Christ into your life or when you decided on a major; or maybe when you realized that life was not always fair. Maybe it was when you finally saw that someone was not being as good to you as you deserved; or maybe it was when you knew the two of you could be friends, but nothing more.

I suppose that all of us have had Odysseus-like experiences in which the truth of something, the direction of something, the clarity of a choice, was seen unambiguously for the first time. These "aha!" moments showed us something and taught us something. And, as a result, our lives were changed.

I think that there *are* moments when God is trying to break through the static with clear communication, or when the Divine is attempting to focus the fuzz and show a fresh perspective. What's at stake is a change, a transformation of our vision—our values, our choices, our direction—and ultimately, our lives.

East coast sociologist and Baptist minister, Dr. Tony Campolo, tells a story of a speaking tour upon which he embarked in a poor corner of the world. As his small two-seater, twin-prop plane was beginning to taxi away from the hangar, a woman from the small village nearby where he had just spoken came running-up to the plane. Pressing her face against the window, she cried out to him, "Here, take my baby. Take my baby." Dr. Campolo looked down, and under her left arm she had a six-month-old girl.

"Take my baby," she repeated, "take my baby. If you don't she'll die here from hunger. If you leave without her, you're killing her."

Prior to this experience, Tony Campolo had preached a lot about salvation, and grace, and heaven. That was the full content of the "good news"—the Gospel—as far as he was concerned: Accept Jesus, live with Jesus in your heart, and your soul will go to heaven.

But this woman was talking about the *present*: "Take my baby *now*," she was saying, "or she is dead!" What does the Gospel have to say to this woman,? Dr. Campolo thought. What does the good news of Jesus Christ mean to the desperate, hungry woman and her ill-fated child in a country where 80% of the children never make it to age 2 due to starvation?

This incident changed Tony Campolo's faith and Tony Campolo's life. It was his descent into hell. Like Odysseus, he emerged out of the experience a transformed Christian. He concluded that he must balance his emphasis on heaven in the afterlife with an emphasis on justice in this life. Was it fair that persons—like small children—died from starvation and disease? What would Jesus say about this? What would Jesus do about this?

As he read the Gospels, Dr. Campolo realized that Jesus was always healing people. Especially as he read and re-read the Gospel of Mark, he came to the insight that Jesus was a miracle worker who cured hurting, diseased, disfigured persons in our world out of compassion. And Tony Campolo's inner-city and international programs launched from his College near Philadelphia, Pennsylvania, are known nation-wide and globally for providing care and healing in a world that is so often cold and diseased.

In Matthew 16, Jesus asks the very profound question, "What does it profit a person if he gains the whole world but forfeits his soul?" Current American culture revolves around the economic, social promise that gaining the whole world is as American as apple pie and as meaningful as it gets. What an acquisitive (not "inquisitive") culture we are!

We are told that our ultimate worth comes from what we have, and our actions should be predicated on the foundation of amassing as much as we can: You only go 'round in life once, so grab all the gusto you can.

This notion of "salvation by shopping alone" stands at sharp odds with the Gospel of Jesus Christ, which reminds us that what counts is your character not your cash, the state of your soul not the credit line on your Visa or MasterCard, and how much and how well you are serving others not how *you* are being served.

I've had a number of experiences which have revealed this to me and questioned the reliability of our cultural values. But I suppose one of the most powerful of these experiences came when I lived in a small village in Nicaragua. This little village, called "San Juan de Limay," was dirt poor—with dirt streets, dirt floors in dirt block houses, and dirty kids accompanied by even dirtier animals. My shower was a water barrel underneath a grape barber, with a cup which served as a showerhead. The bathroom was a hole behind a big rock out back, and my bedroom was shared with a couple baby pigs who refused to stay outside the house but instead had the regrettable and sleep-disturbing habit of cuddling-up beside me!

In the midst of this situation, I thought of my own home in the U.S., my paycheck from teaching college (my host made $500 a year), my family doctor whose prenatal care, birthing room, postnatal care and vaccines had enabled my own two children to be healthy and to have a future.

What does the Gospel of Jesus Christ have to say to the poverty in which Manuel, Rosa, and their children lived?, I pondered. And what "good news" gave these persons hope?, I wondered. And could I learn something about my Christian faith and my Christian walk *from* these people, as well as provide something *to* them?

I think that I learned from them that poverty *is* a form of violence, perhaps the worst kind (as Gandhi once said); I've had revealed to me that when Jesus said, "Blessed are the poor in spirit," he meant that poor persons have no one or no thing to depend on except God; whereas, you and I often get distracted by our things, our plenty, and our acquisitions, which at times insulate us from our real and ultimate dependence on God and our awareness of just how much we count on God. I've had the flash in insight that says that those of us who are "haves" must share our abundance with those who have little or nothing at all, for that is what Jesus would do—that is what Jesus *did* do!

Living in Nicaragua was for me a descent into hell. Like Odysseus, like Tony Campolo, it transformed me into a changed person: What does it profit a person if she gains the whole world but forfeits her soul?

Well, how many of you have a trip planned to Hades soon? How many of you have reservations on a two-engine small plane to go to a remote corner of the globe? How many of you are packing your bags for a little village on the border between Nicaragua and Honduras?

But this fall semester you are going to be in classes and lectures and assigned readings which can expose you to topics you have never thought-of before, which can take you to places you have never been before, which can propel you to face issues that may trouble you, confound you, and even depress you. And you can be in Bible studies and spiritual life groups that bring fresh ideas and novel perspectives to bear on the familiar and the unfamiliar.

And religious gatherings on campus will at times broach the boundaries of the controversial, the upsetting, even the taboo. But if we can't think about the tough topics here in college, and we can't ask the tough questions here at this College, where *can* we do this?

But all of this is okay, I think: For an education in a church-related college offers, and should be offering, opportunities for those descents into hell which can inform us, influence us, change us, transform us—all for the better!

So, this academic year, I wish for all of us occasions and opportunities which can positively enlarge our knowledge and positively impact our faith. I wish for all of us, descents into Hades. Now hear me clearly: I did not just tell you all to 'go to hell'! Rather, I am saying to you that our descents into "hell," like Odysseus' descent into Hades, can be some of the most enlightening and most enriching experiences of our lives.

For what *does* it profit a person if he gains the whole world but forfeits his soul?

Scripture for reflection: Matthew 16:24-26; Mark 8:34-37

Apollo or Dionysus?

When I was a college student, there were persons called "Ralston Straight Shooters." These persons took rules and regulations to the max.—no fun, no games, just strict discipline, more don't's than do's, playing it close, no wobbles, no compromises, no accommodation. Straight and narrow, the Ralston Straight Shooters.

In the ancient world, the god Apollo was a Ralston Straight Shooter. The most handsome and best loved of the twelve great gods of Greece, Apollo was the god of light and of manliness.

Apollo was also the enemy of all things bad and ugly. He came from Mt. Olympus brandishing a silver bow and a quiver with golden arrows, which he used to kill evil things like the deadly serpent, Python.

Apollo was also a guardian god and a health-giving god. In his "spare time," he was also the god of song, music, and poetry.

All-in-all, Apollo was pretty cool—in an uptight, *restrained* way. The emperor, Caesar Augustus, regarded Apollo as his patron deity and built a magnificent temple in his honor. Apollo, and for that matter Caesar as well, were for "law and order." Apollo represented the straight and narrow. Apollo stood for discipline. Apollo was a Ralston Straight Shooter.

When I was a college student, there were also persons who were called Party Animals. These persons cast-off conformity to the rules, followed the lead of basic appetites, and "partied hearty"—more do's than don't's, playing loose, anything's possible, letting go, getting crazy, going wild, the Party Animals.

In the ancient world, the god Dionysus was a Party Animal. The son of Zeus (god of the sky) and Semele (goddess of the earth), Dionysus was the god of the vine and the growing principle of nature. Riding in a chariot drawn by lions and leopards, he was attended by a dancing "bevy of bodacious babes" ("so many women, so little time"). Dionysus roamed the earth teaching people how to cultivate grapes and make wine.

All-in-all, Dionysus was a cool dude—in an uncontrolled, *bohemian* way. A lover of fun, Dionysus was out for a good time. Dionysus—wild and crazy. Dionysus stood for celebration. Dionysus was a Party Animal.

You and I probably know Christians who fall into the two extremes of the Ralston Straight Shooter and the Party Animal, the extremes of Apollo and Dionysus, the extremes of "rigid discipline" and "unbridled celebration."

I remember "Amy," who was so picky and uptight about her Christian faith that she wasn't much fun to be around. She worried that every little shortcoming or imperfection she saw in herself was absolute proof that she had committed the "unforgivable sin." Plus, she was convinced that everyone—save the persons that went to her dad's church—who disagreed with her were immoral and destined for the fires of hell!

Amy was Apollo in Christian dress (actually *a* Christian dress, for she thought that pants were unfeminine and unchristian).

On the other hand, I remember "Mark," who was always at all the parties, usually slamming down some brewskies . . . a *lot* of brewskies, I recall! He told the funniest, most politically-incorrect and inappropriate jokes I have ever heard.

Mark was Dionysus become intoxicated by the spirits.

Apollo and Dionysus. Discipline and celebration.

Sometimes, Christian history reveals a one-sided, extreme emphasis on either Apollo or Dionysus. While one may be impressed by the spiritual depth expressed in the writings of the Desert Fathers of the early Church, one may also be shocked by their excesses—self-deprivations that went far beyond "fasting to cleanse the soul," and self-flagellation that involved whipping themselves or beating themselves with sticks, and even castration!

Such austerity did not end in the formative years of the Church, but continued, for example, even in "jolly old England" (which apparently was not always so "jolly"): In the sixteenth century, a law was passed which forbade any merriment at all during the Christmas season. Advent was to be observed with a penitent, sober awareness on the part of Christians of their personal sins which made necessary the entry of the Christ-child into the world.

Further, Christmas Day itself was to be spent in quiet, disciplined confession of all shortcomings—both great and small—in each individual. In fact, soldiers were dispersed to roam the neighborhoods, ensuring that no turkeys were being cooked in stoves and no celebrative Christmas dinners were being eaten. It would not only be immoral and unchristian to do so, but also illegal.

And in Scotland in the nineteenth century, a young minister was brought before his presbytery for ice-skating on Sunday from one appointment to another. One member of the presbytery fixed a stern eye on him and demanded, "Tell me, young man, did ye *enjoy* the skating?"

At times, the excesses of Apollo have prevailed.

At other times, the Dionysian extreme has prevailed. In his ministry to the churches of the Gentile world, the Apostle Paul often had to discipline, correct, even scold, some of the church members for their beliefs and practices. In the church in Corinth, Greece, for example, some members were taking the Holy Communion celebration a bit *too* celebratively and without sufficient holiness. As a matter of fact, the services had degenerated into drunken orgies. That's why Paul chastised them and told them that this abomination could not continue. Celebration without any constraint at all was not Christian.

Such indulgence did not end with the first-century churches, but continued, for example, in religious excitement that became fanaticism in the medieval Crusades and in the uncontrolled zeal of the thirteenth-century Inquisition.

At times, the excesses of Dionysus have prevailed.

In the New Testament, we see Jesus taking a position right in the center between Apollo and Dionysus. Like Aristotle in the West and the Buddha in the East, Jesus walked the middle path between the two extremes of "stifling discipline" and "excessive celebration."

On the one hand, Jesus knew the need for moral discipline. He knew how important it was to obey God and to pursue righteousness. So when the Spirit of God nudged him, he was led into the wilderness to be tempted, as the Gospel of Luke says, "for forty days" (4:2). During this time, Jesus undertook the spiritual and physical rigor of fasting. The Apostle Paul described Jesus as "obedient, even to death on a cross" (Philippians 2:8).

At the same time, Jesus recognized that an extreme devotion to discipline could squeeze out joy and celebration. Jesus knew that an emphasis on Apollo with no creative tension with Dionysus could be dangerous.

For that reason, he criticized his fellow Jews—the scribes and Pharisees—for getting too caught-up at times in the *letter* of ethical discipline and in the process losing a sense of the uplifting *spirit* of morality. Obedience with no joy, Apollo with no counterbalancing of Dionysus, leads to an oppressed, not liberated, life.

And so, at the wedding feast of Cana, Jesus was willing to respond to a dilemma, a problem, which if uncorrected would result in tremendous embarrassment for the bride and groom: The wine had run out.

Hospitality was, and still is, a sacred duty in the Middle East. Not having adequate provisions for guests violates a crucial social custom. So, when the wine ran out at the wedding feast in Cana of Galilee, this was a substantial problem. Jesus responded by changing some jars of water into wine. In fact, he changed a *lot* of water into a *lot* of wine. And by so doing, embarrassment was avoided, and the celebration could continue.

Jesus was no killjoy. But at the same time, he was no relentless Dionysian. He knew what would follow concerning the wine, and what would follow was this: Jewish custom dictated that the wine be mixed with water—specifically, two parts wine would be added to three parts water. In this way, the alcohol content of the wine was diluted, thus ensuring that the wedding guests would not become drunk. Wine was necessary for a wedding celebration, but intoxication was not to be tolerated.

In the social *mores* of Israel, drunkenness was a moral, religious, and public embarrassment. The Book of Proverbs puts it powerfully:

> Do not be among winebibbers or among gluttonous eaters of meat . . . [for] wine bites like a serpent and stings like a poisonous snake. (23:20, 32)

In fact, when Jesus' opponents wanted to try to chip-away at his public image and reputation (since they had had no success at all in public debate with him), they accused him of being a "winebibber and a gluttonous man" (Matthew 11:19). My point here is not to defend Jesus against such character defamation, but rather to indicate that such a charge points to what a public *disgrace* being a drunkard and a pig was.

So, in Jesus we see a person who was neither a Ralston Straight Shooter nor a Party Animal, neither a straight-laced Apollonarian nor an unrestrained Dionysian.

I invite you to think of our Christian journey in terms of the discipline of Apollo and the celebration of Dionysus. Standing midway between the extremes of self-mortification and self-indulgence places us in creative tension between Apollo and Dionysus, between being a Ralston Straight Shooter and a Party Animal. It places us in

A User-friendly Universe?

the middle with Christ. It places us in Christ. It places Christ in us. May this close relationship with Jesus Christ provide us with illumination, instruction, and inspiration.

Scripture for reflection: Proverbs 23:19-21, 29-35; John 2:1-11

Take Courage!

Storms come up quickly on the Sea of Galilee. A Jewish writer, a contemporary of Jesus, described it in this way: "It is not unusual to see terrible squalls hurl themselves, even when the sky is perfectly clear, upon these waters which are ordinarily so calm."

I have had first-hand experience of this abrupt change—one moment this lake by Tiberias in Israel can be still, calm, and sunny, the next, windy, choppy, and dark. I would liken it to what people often say about the state in which they live in the U.S.: "If you don't like the weather here, just wait a minute, and it will change!"

The weather changed on the disciples and Jesus. Jesus was riding in the boat in the stern, sleeping on a pillow. This would be an honored position, one in which any special person would be transported. Ancient sources tell us that "in these boats . . . the place for any distinguished person was on the little seat placed at the stern, where a carpet and cushion were arranged." So, according to this custom, Jesus was seated at the rear of the boat, catching some rest.

Jesus was then urgently roused by his fellow passengers, who were frightened by the storm that suddenly and disturbingly swept upon them. In fact, they were so fearful that they shouted to Jesus, "Don't you care if we drown?"

Jesus stood up in the boat and rebuked the wind and said to the waves, "Quiet! Be still!"—much in the same way that a grade school teacher would try to regain order and restore calm in the classroom.

Much to the relief of the terrified disciples, the wind died down, and everything was still, just as it had been before.

I find it interesting that the words which Jesus addressed to the wind and the waves are the exact same words that he spoke to the demon-possessed man in Mark 1:25—"Be quiet!" The reason for the duplication is not that Jesus was deficient in vocabulary or needed a course in public speaking. Rather, the words are the same because people in Jesus' time believed that the destructive power of storms was due to the evil activity of demons in nature, just as they believed that mental-psychological disorders in people were due to the presence and power of demons in the human personality.

I have always been moved by this story of Jesus' calming the storm. I think that it shows forth not only the power of Jesus as one who has authority over the forces of nature, but also the compassion of Jesus as he immediately responds to the fears of the passengers.

And yet, I fear that we do this episode in Jesus' ministry an injustice if we regard it too much as a single, historical occurrence. If we look upon the silencing of the wind and waves—as wonderful and as marvelous a story as it is—as simply a physical miracle which Jesus performed, then we make it into something that happened once, a long time ago, in a faraway place, in the northern region of a small country in an outlying province of the Roman Empire.

But if we see the story in a symbolic sense, it seems to hold even more value for our Christian faith and for our lives of discipleship today. When the disciples realized the presence of Jesus with them—when they remembered he was along with them for the journey and when they appealed to him—the storm became calm. Once they were reassured that he was riding with them as a fellow passenger and certainly did not want them to be drowned, there was a calm, fearless peace in their hearts no matter what the sudden storm was like.

To have Jesus as the distinguished Guest in their boat—to have Jesus as the special Friend in one's life—was to travel with courage even in a storm. I think that that's true today, just as it was true back then. It's true here, just as it was true in Palestine. And it's true not just once, but in every time. The calming of the storm is something that still happens, and it is something that can happen for *us*! In the presence of Jesus, we can have courage and peace in even the wildest and most frightening storms of life.

The writer, Dorothy Bernard, has written, "Courage is fear that has said its prayers."

No person have I known as completely fearless. Even Jesus, who resolutely "set his face toward Jerusalem" (according to the Bible) asked in the Garden of Gethsemane that the cup of death might pass from him (if it were God's will), and on the cross on Good Friday he cried out at what at least appeared to him to be abandonment: "My God, my God, why have you forsaken me?" (Psalm 22:1).

In fact, fear can function in a healthy manner for us. Without valid fear, a person would be prone to run headlong into unavoidable danger. Such a person could cause injury, sickness, or even death, to one's self, or to others. Healthy fear of disease has produced scientific medicine. Fear of ignorance is responsible for educational systems. Healthy fear (or at least, respect) for bodies of water has led to greater safety measures in boating, swimming, and sailing. Fear of terrorism has led to greater vigilance on the part of citizens and to the creation of Homeland Security.

Fear of what environmental degradation can do to our planet home (and to all its inhabitants, including us humans) has led to some constructive steps toward sustainability and stability. Fear of poverty led years ago to the creation of Social Security for the retired and to minimum wage laws and today to the ideal of universal health coverage. Fear of what moral failure and spiritual loss create has often led to our search for God, and God's search for us, and God's costly gift of what theological vocabulary calls "grace" and "salvation."

My point is this: Fear may play a useful, even healthy, role. Courage is not the absence of fear; it is the control of it. I think this is part of what the philosopher Aristotle meant when he positioned courage as the mean between the two extremes of foolhardiness and cowardice. The foolhardy person rushes-in with no sensitivity to the price that may be paid; the foolhardy person has no fear, and this person is not to be envied. The cowardly person never rushes in, regardless of the importance of the action; the cowardly person has been mastered by fear.

But a courageous person, in contrast to both extremes, realistically fears what may be involved or what may result; but that person is not deterred from action and involvement, when involvement and action are warranted and necessary. The courageous person acts and is not inactive; but the courageous person acts wisely and not foolishly.

Courage is fear that has said its prayers. Jesus says, "Take courage!; for I am with you."

Courage—along with wisdom, temperance, justice, faith, hope, and love—has been considered by the Church for centuries as one of the seven cardinal virtues. Scottish writer, James M. Barrie, the author of *Peter Pan*, told students in an address, "Courage is the lovely virtue . . . courage is the thing. All goes if courage goes."

The eminent theologian, Paul Tillich, himself an example of courage in Nazi Germany and in his forced exile to the United States, wrote a wonderful book entitled, *The Courage To Be*. Originally delivered as the Terry Lectures at Yale University, *The Courage To Be* discusses the meaning of courage in the history of Western thought and where courage comes from.

Dr. Tillich provides a perceptive analysis of "fear" in his discussion of courage. He used a word which runs much deeper than fear—"anxiety"—but there is a certain degree of carryover. What I find particularly interesting, and what is especially pertinent to a consideration of "fear" and "courage," is his generalization of the fears and anxieties of particular historical periods. He makes three such generalizations:

In the Middle Ages, there was especially prevalent a fear of death. There were, of course, other fears as well; but the one which predominated was the fear of a person's ceasing to be. I'm suspicious that lethal diseases and short life spans were partial "fuels for the fire." Who wouldn't worry about death, with the bubonic plague at its greatest lethal impact contributing 100 corpses each day to one church's funeral schedule? So, medieval persons feared death as a threat to their living, to their very "being."

In the Reformation, there was especially prevalent a fear of guilt. There were, of course, other fears as well—the fear of death, for example, seems universally present. But the one fear which predominated was the fear of moral condemnation for one's sins and shortcomings. Since, as Paul writes in Romans, "All have sinned and fall short of the glory of God" (3:23), no one was exempt from potentially feeling guilt and condemnation for inevitable sinning.

In modern times, there seems especially prevalent a fear of meaninglessness. There are, of course, other fears as well—the fear of death continues to drive persons to seek personal immortality, sometimes through bequests to institutions for buildings and programs, sometimes through offspring enjoying hefty inheritances. And for the majority today, there is a recognition that we are not perfectly nor fully the virtuous people God would have us be; for a minority, the weight of moral commissions and omissions presses them into low self-esteem, even neurosis. But the one fear which seems to predominate, says Dr. Tillich, is the fear that one's life has no purpose, that there may be no meaning to life at all. What if it's all been for nought?

I think these questions nip at us today: Tragedies which too-often occur in our society and in the world remind us of our mortality. We may truly believe that "whether we live or whether we die, we are the Lord's" (Romans 14:8b); yet which of us would not want to live longer before we go to be with God?

And our gridlock in Washington, D.C.—despite elections which always seem to be rolling around—may produce fears that corruption, partisan politics, and greed will prevail no matter who is in office. "The more that things change, the more they remain the same." I am reminded that in the ancient world, the statues of emperors and other high officials had removable heads. When one emperor died or was deposed, only the head was taken-off; the body remained to receive the bust of the new emperor. I confess that I sometimes fear that no matter who the political faces are, the body politic remains the same.

And in the midst of our seemingly interminable busyness—with infinite things to accomplish in finite time, and with countless duties beyond description—we may question whether our lives are meaningful or not!

"Take courage!; for I am with you." There is divine presence to speak to our fear of death. There is divine forgiveness to absolve us of our sins. There is divine guidance to restore our sense of purpose.

Life, like the Sea of Galilee, can subject us to sudden storms. Even when it seems calm and sunny, harsh winds and driving rain and rough waves may suddenly erupt and rock our boat. But we are not alone in our journey. Because Jesus is with us and does not want us to drown, because the power of God is with us to calm the storm, and because the Spirit is with us to give us peace, we can take courage.

Courage is fear that has said its prayers. Take courage!; for Jesus is with you. Take courage!; for Christ goes with you. Take courage!

Scripture for reflection: Mark 4:35-41

Ahadun and the Three Golden Calves

What is the fastest growing religion in the world today? If you said, "Christianity," you would be incorrect (even though almost one of every three persons on planet Earth is Christian).

If you said, "Judaism," you would also be incorrect. Judaism is the smallest of the world religions, at 12-14 million, and thus only a tiny percentage of the world's population.

If you said, "Islam," you would be absolutely correct. Islam is the fastest growing religion on the planet, with 1 in every 5 persons claiming submission to *Allah,* the Arabic word for God.

One of my favorite Muslim stories comes from the very beginning of the emergence of Islam in Saudi Arabia. As Islam began to grow in the 7th century Arabian peninsula, it met resistance, hostility, and persecution (P.S. The same thing happened to Christianity in its early years in the Roman Empire). The resistance took the form of laughter, the hostility the form of stones thrown, and the persecution the form of prison or death.

These negative reactions were indeed negative because Islam advocated a strict, rigid monotheism (or belief in *one* God). That is, Islam holds that there is a single God, and persons do not choose to worship that God as a choice in opposition to other gods. No, Islam says there really is only one God and that persons choose either to worship that one God or none at all.

One non-Muslim merchant owned a slave who had converted to Islam. So strong in his faith was this slave and so unwilling to compromise, that the master out of anger and frustration combined, took the slave to the desert, staked him out in the sand, put a large, smooth stone on his chest, and waited for the sun to take its toll. As the sun rose from morning to high noon, the stone on the slave's chest got hotter and hotter. And the man's flesh started burning worse and worse and worse.

The slave's master thought, 'At last this stubborn, obstinate slave will recant and cast-off his Muslim faith.' But, to his surprise and simultaneous dismay, the slave would not. Even though he was cooking to death out in the desert heat, he would not renounce his commitment to Islam. All he would say was *ahadun, ahadun, ahadun*. This cry in the Arabic language means, "one [God], one [God], one [God]."

In final desperation, the Muslim slave's master sold him to another merchant, this one a Muslim!

In a scripture passage from the Jewish prophet Isaiah, God is proclaimed to be the first, the last, the only. God is the Alpha, God is the Omega, God alone is God—there is no other. This proclamation, of course, came over a thousand years before Islam began.

This view that there is only ONE GOD has determined Western notions of divinity for centuries. Every Jewish worship service begins with the *Shema*, the confession of one God from Deuteronomy 6:

Shema, Yisrael, Adonai eloheynu, Adonai echad.

[In translation from the Hebrew]: "Hear O Israel, the Lord is God, the Lord is one."

In the history of religion on planet earth, people have originally and typically worshipped the various forces of nature and the spirits of ancestors. The wind, rain, sun, moon, thunder, and lightning were all worshipped as individual gods, and the spirits of departed grandparents, aunts and uncles, and parents were all revered and placated, lest you get on their bad side, and calamities result. In fact, in Hinduism—the oldest world religion (perhaps excluding indigenous religions such as Native American traditions)—there are believed to be 330 million gods. There is one function for every god, and one god for each function. Depending on your need, you might worship one particular god from the horde of available gods at a certain, given time.

In contrast, in Judaism and Islam, and Christianity as well, there is what I would call a "divine economy": In monotheism, the belief in just one God (not one among many, but just one in total), God fulfills a multitude of functions. It's one God, many functions, not many gods with one function for each. As Isaiah puts it, "There is but one God, and besides him, there is no other."

Ahadun [one (God)] means that there can be no other. If we say, claim, confess, that "we believe in God, the Father almighty, Maker of heaven and earth" (from the Apostles' Creed), then only God is worthy of being our top priority and is deserving of our praise and worship.

Ahadun. The worst sin for a Muslim is idolatry—that is, worshipping as God something that is less than God. The Arabic word for idolatry is *shirk*. We English-speakers have borrowed that Arabic word, *shirk*, and placed it into our vocabulary. We say that someone has "shirked" an important duty or "shirked" a promised responsibility.

Muslims say the same thing, but about God. To "shirk" is to forget that there is only one God, that the only divinity is the Almighty, that the only reality we ought to be worshipping is God. To worship other than God is to "shirk."

Of course, the Israelites engaged in "major 'shirk'" back in the 13th century B.C. You and I remember it as the "Golden Calf fiasco." Moses ascends to the top of Mt. Sinai to get the rules of the covenant from the God of the covenant. When he descends, the Israelites—who have been liberated by this God of the covenant from indentured servitude in the construction business—have constructed a calf made of gold. This clearly was idol worship, as the calf or bull was a symbol of fertility in the ancient Near East. The Israelites were worshipping some reality other than the one reality which alone deserved to be worshipped. Moses, as a result, "went ballistic," and broke the tablets, for the Israelites had "shirked" their responsibility as covenant children of the one God. Rather than giving thanks to God for what God had done by worshipping God alone, they had flirted with other gods and worshipped them.

Naturally, it is comfortable for you and me to point accusing, self-righteous fingers at the Israelites and smugly shout out, "You sinful, unfaithful, ungrateful, sniveling Israelites. How could you have done such a thing? I mean, after God had done so much for you in terms of your Exodus from Egypt. What fickle, opportunistic, untrustworthy blockheads!"

But, what a minute. Don't we, too, at times chase "golden calves" of our own creation? Don't we sometimes shirk our monotheistic faith because of the temptation of some other thing, some other reality, to take center stage or be elevated as top priority? Don't we occasionally fail in our thanksgiving by worshipping "other-than-God"?

I would suggest three such "golden calves" (perhaps you can think of others as well):

The first golden calf I would accent is self-worship. Instead of God, we worship ourselves. Instead of obeying God's will, we give-in to our own. Rather than resolving with Jesus, "Not my will but yours be done," we proclaim, "Not your will but mine be done."

This self-worship places us, not God, at the center of our personal universes. What matters is my happiness, my situation, my satisfaction, my pleasure, period. I worship myself, I love myself, I think only of my own self-interest.

Self-worship, self-love, egoism, is a golden calf for which we shirk our devotion to *Ahadun*, one God.

This first golden calf is worshipping self rather than God, or egoism.

The second golden calf I would suggest is nation-worship. We Americans are quite fortunate to have the opportunities and life-style and upward mobility that are available in the United States. We certainly have great freedom and flexibility here: Depending on our gifts, our work ethic, and (okay, to be realistic) our connections, we can rise to fulfill our deepest ambitions.

This situation rightly calls forth a high level of loyalty to our country. We commonly call this "patriotism." Patriotism is okay.

But sometimes patriotism escalates into what we may call "nationalism" or a worship of the nation as God. In this situation, the nation can do no wrong and anyone who criticizes the United States is a bona fide "Benedict Arnold" who deserves ridicule if not deportation and exile.

A "patriot" is appreciative, and may at times be critical. A "nationalist" is blindly loyal and refuses to concede any national shortcoming. The nation is not merely appreciated, it is worshipped. The country is not simply enjoyed, it is regarded as infallible (that is, incapable of error). U.S. citizens in this view are seen only as superiors, as a contemporary "chosen people," with whom God especially connects and resides, with whom God has a unique stake, and whom God distinctively favors.

This is nationalism, not patriotism, and it hinges on worship—the worship of the country. Nation-worship or nationalism is a second golden calf.

The third golden calf that occurs to me is dollar-worship or materialism. To say that we are a materialistic culture is an understatement. Our standard of living is among the highest in the world; our natural resources, though not inexhaustible, are not overall in scarce supply; our possessions are numerous and important to us.

In fact, we are a consumer-driven society. Acquisitiveness is built in: If we can just have the right thing or the "top of the line" model or the best smelling brand or the most efficient product or the latest craze, if we can amass the right quantity of this and the largest number of that, if we can just do all this, we will be envied, respected, and happy (in fact, our lives will be ultimately happy

A User-friendly Universe?

and "epic"). Personal meaning and fulfillment—according to the mantra of a materialistic society—lie in the quantity of your goods and possessions not the growth of your soul.

The first golden calf is self-worship or egoism.

The second golden calf is nation-worship or nationalism.

The third golden calf is dollar-worship or materialism.

If we truly want to give to God our thanks for what God has done for us, if we deeply desire to show our appreciation to God for God's many blessings, then we must decide to resist the temptation to worship those things which promise us fulfillment and meaning, but deliver fraud and disappointment.

To the golden calves with which we flirt, we must shout out, *Ahadun* [One ([God)].

For "thus says the Lord: I am the first and last, I am the only one. Besides me, there is no other." *Ahadun. Ahadun.*

Scripture for reflection: Deuteronomy 6:4-6; Isaiah 44:6-8; Exodus 32:1-4

Masks

"Trick or Treat?" they say to me when they stop by my door. "Trick or Treat?" they ask me, and then challenge me to guess who they are. Those little neighborhood tricksters take particular delight in stumping me regarding their identities. In fact, I'm not sure I can normally keep them straight anyway, not to mention in costumes and with masks on!

Masks have a long history. It's probably a toss-up as to whether they were first used to conceal the identities of robbers or to reveal the identities of various characters played by actors on the ancient stage. If part of the costume of bandits, masks hid the identities of assailants who intended to remain unknown. If part of theatrical wardrobe, then the masks clearly pointed to various personalities in the comedy or tragedy. Indeed, a few actors could play a whole cast of characters simply by wearing different masks at various times and thereby moving from role to role within the play.

Masks, then, can either hide or reveal a character's identity. If intended to conceal that identity, a mask disguises what is underneath. The external impression it gives is false and misleading; the internal reality is much different from what it appears to be on the outside.

In a family argument amongst Jews, Jesus chastises the scribes and Pharisees for their inconsistent behavior. In fact, Jesus jumps on their case with seven charges, each one beginning with the word, "woe": "Woe to you scribes and Pharisees, for you lock people out of the kingdom of heaven"; "woe to you scribes and Pharisees, for you tithe, but you have neglected the more important matters of Torah—namely justice, mercy and faith"; "woe to you scribes and Pharisees, for outwardly you appear one way, but on the inside you are full of self-indulgence and greed"; "woe to you scribes and Pharisees, for you are like whitewashed tombs, beautiful on the outside, but on the inside full of death and filth—you look righteous on the outside, but on the inside you are full of hypocrisy and immorality."

Jesus' simile of "whitewashed tombs" would have been particularly poignant to persons of his day. But the simile loses substantial power when we try to carry it forward two millennia to the 21st century. In Jesus' time, one of the most common locations for tombs was by the highways and byways that crisscrossed Palestine. These tombs were off-limits, according to Jewish "law" (teaching), because anyone who came into contact with them (i.e., with death) was rendered unclean. This was especially the case for religious rituals, and an "unclean" person could not participate in Jewish ceremonies.

At one time in particular during the year, the roads were overcrowded with religious pilgrims. This was the time of the Passover celebration, the joyous remembrance of the deliverance of the Israelites from Egyptian slavery. If a person were to become unclean on his way to *Pesach* (the Passover), this would be a terrible tragedy, for he would be forbidden to participate in this extremely sacred and moving spiritual celebration.

As a result, it became a regular practice during the Jewish month of *Adar* (a month in the springtime) to whitewash all roadside tombs, so that no religious pilgrims might accidentally come into contact with them and be rendered unclean. So, as an individual journeyed the roads of Palestine on a March or April day, these tombs would glint bright white, almost dazzlingly beautiful, in the sunshine. But within, the tombs would be full of bones and bodies whose touch would defile.

"A whitewashed tomb," declared Jesus, was a precise picture of what the scribes and Pharisees had become. Though their outward behaviors seemed to be the actions of intensely religious persons, their inward hearts were tainted and filled with unhealthy motives.

Some biblical scholars refer to this section of Matthew 23 as "the most forceful and most sustained denunciation of any group in the whole New Testament" (e.g., Dr. A.T. Robinson). And recall that Jesus, Jewish by birth and by religion, is criticizing fellow Jews. What seems to spur Jesus' tirade is the inconsistency between outward appearance and inward reality. How deceitful it is to give an external impression that camouflages an internal disposition!

Jesus calls the scribes and Pharisees (and anyone else, for that matter) on this inconsistency. He frequently uses the term "hypocrite" to designate those who give one impression while masking their true intention. I find Jesus' use of the word interesting: The original word which translates as "hypocrite" is the Greek, *hupokrites*. *Hupokrites* literally meant "one who answers" and was connected with the statement-and-answer—the dialogue—of the theater stage. In fact, *hupokrites* is the regular Greek word for "actor."

The way in which Jesus used the word suggests that the scribes and Pharisees were actors in the worst sense of the term—pretenders, those who simply acted a part without truly living it, those who wore masks to cover their true feelings, those who put on an external "show" while inwardly their thought and feelings were very different, and quite contradictory.

This can still happen, and does. As William Shakespeare articulated it, "A man may smile and smile and be a villain." A person may wear a mask which disguises, but does not transform.

Casey Stengel was a colorful baseball manager of the New York Yankees. He was also a stickler for rules. While his team was undergoing spring training in St. Petersburg, Florida, Mr. Stengel approached the elevator in the hotel late one night (this was back in the days when elevators weren't run by buttons but by an elevator operator). Pulling a baseball out of his pocket, he told the operator, "I gotta give this ball to a kid at tomorrow's pre-season game. Do me a favor, will ya? If any of my players come-in after me, get them to sign this ball and give it to me at breakfast, okay?" The elevator operator agreed. The next morning, Casey Stengel was the first person at breakfast, and the elevator operator handed him the ball. It had four or five signatures of Yankee players who had come-in later than Stengel the night before. Mr. Stengel took the ball, thanked the elevator operator, and promptly fined all the players who'd signed the ball, for breaking the team's curfew.

The baseball masked the true intent of the manager. The elevator operator took it, believing that the signatures on the ball were needed in order to give some kid the thrill of a lifetime. The Yankee players signed the ball, believing at face value that they were doing something nice. All of them were taken-in by a seemingly-innocent act which had ulterior motives.

It was clear that the scribes and Pharisees revealed ulterior, hypocritical motives. They acted one way, but were on the inside another way. But before we join confidently and perhaps arrogantly in their chastisement, let us pause in humility and honesty: As the old saying goes, "People who live in glass houses should not throw stones." Or, as Jesus put it to the crowd who wanted to follow faithfully the commandment of Torah and punish by stoning to death the woman caught in adultery, "Let the person who has never sinned throw the first rock."

So let's be realistic, let's get real, about ourselves: We are not always the people we pretend to be; we are never fully the persons we wish we were. All of us are a mixture of "saint" and "sinner." At times, we are kind and considerate; at times, we are forgiving and patient; at times we are other-directed and loving of our neighbor. But at other times, we are irritable and resentful; at other times, we are fuming and seeking retaliation; at other times, we are impatient, self-absorbed, and envious of our neighbor.

In some cases, perhaps too many cases, we say one thing and do another. Or, we do a thing which on the surface appears to be one way, but in truth it is quite deceitful or insidious. In other words, we are quite human, sometimes more-so rather than less-so.

Therefore, we know that we are always in need of God's grace and Christ's redemption. Indeed, God's forgiveness and Christ's giving us "second chances" are absolutely crucial for our accepting ourselves as creatures who occasionally—sometimes regularly—screw-up.

I like theologian Paul Tillich's words here: "Just accept the fact that you are accepted." That is, simply affirm yourself as one who has been forgiven by God through God's grace, no matter what unpleasant or unacceptable thing you have done.

I also like the Apostle Paul's words here: "We know that a person is justified not by the works of the law [the commandments of Torah] but through faith in Jesus Christ" (Galatians 2:16).

Sometimes we wear masks to disguise our true intentions. We are hypocrites, for the way we seem is not the way that we truly are.

But I think that there is yet another way in which we wear masks. I think that each of us is not only a mixture of "saint and sinner," but also a mixture of "self-confidence and self-doubt." That is, on the one hand, we acknowledge to ourselves that we possess some God-given gifts—we all have some talents and abilities. Thanks be to God that God has graciously presented us with certain potentials, specific dispositions, special knacks, that we may develop and polish.

But, on the other hand, we all carry some measure of a lack of self-assurance. We all know that we have shortcomings, for who is perfect? If you say you are perfect, then you are not, for you have committed the sin of pride! And we all have anxieties and doubt whether we can really get the job done.

I think that that is why we sometimes wear masks—to disguise our insecurities, to keep persons at a distance so that they will not get close enough to see the real "us." Because if persons get too close, they will see our weaknesses, our deficiencies, and our flaws and foibles (which we all have). So, in a sense, and to different degrees, we walk around with masks on, trying to camouflage our vulnerability, worrying about our insecurities, and wondering "Will people like me?"

A User-friendly Universe?

God, of course, sees through all this like no other. God knows us as no other does. Martin Luther recognized this and celebrated it five centuries ago when he valued the 139th Psalm as his favorite:

> O Lord, you have searched me and known me . . .
> You discern my thoughts from afar . . .
> You are acquainted with all my ways.
> Even before a word is on my tongue, O Lord,
> you know it completely . . .
> Search me, O God, and know my heart;
> Test me and know my thoughts.
> See if there is any wicked way in me,
> And lead me in the life everlasting.

This great reformer, who believed that God knew him completely and thoroughly, nailed his Ninety-five Theses for Debate on the door of the castle church at Wittenberg, an act which gave rise to the Protestant Reformation. The date was October 31st, 1517, the evening before All Saints' Day, "Halloween."

I wonder how many interesting and life-enriching persons we miss getting to know because of the masks that they wear and the masks that we wear. Their insecurities and our insecurities feed each other and keep us at a distance. Are there people around us that we could benefit from knowing better?

I overheard a conversation at a small airport in Virginia that involved an individual who needed to recognize and know better another person. When a woman arrived at the gate for an early morning flight to Baltimore, there was no one at the check-in desk. Then a fellow in an airline uniform walked to the gate's jet-way and tried several times, unsuccessfully, to enter the proper sequence of numbers to unlock the door. Next, he went behind the desk and began clicking away at the computer.

Thinking that this person could assist her, the woman approached the desk and looked over to the man. "I don't know the new code for the jet-way," he said bluntly. "I can't get this computer to work, and I'm not able to help you." Assuming that a bit of humor might help, the woman said, "Are we having a bad day this morning?" "You'd better hope not," came the reply, "I'm your pilot!"

We might benefit from getting to know better, people we don't know at all! And we might even benefit from getting to know better the people we already think we know.

Masks. Let us vow to mesh our words and deeds and avoid the "white-washed tomb syndrome." May God's grace and Christ's example guide and inspire us.

Masks. Let us vow to reach out to others risking our vulnerabilities and insecurities and thereby have our lives, and the lives of others, enriched. May God's courage and Christ's example empower and direct us.

Scripture for reflection: Psalm 139:1-14, 23-24; Matthew 23:1-11, 23-28

Why Are *We* Blessed?

Thanksgiving has always been a very special holiday for me: When I was growing up, the Cain family always had a celebration at this time of the year especially. How I remember the good food, the laughter, the teasing, the sharing of family stories, and the tv blaring incessantly in the family room with a football game.

Thanksgiving will be quite different at the Ortiz house in Central America. The corn crop has failed (too little rain), so the tortillas will be fewer in number. There will be a tiny scrap of meat, enough rice for one small helping each, and some refried beans. The food will smell and taste good, but the menu will be no different from any other day. Several of the children will opt to sit on the dirt floor, cross-legged, their metal plates perched precariously on their tiny laps.

Thanksgiving will be different still at Amusiri's house in Africa. Amusiri had several brothers and sisters, but all but one are dead now—first tuberculosis hit, then malaria broke-out, and finally the famine came. Only the hardiest children had any chance at all, and Amusiri's mother was forced to give the meager amounts of food to the children who had the best chance of making it. Amusiri will eat on Thanksgiving, but it won't be much, and it won't be enough. And yes, she'll go to bed Thanksgiving night with her stomach growling and with those persistent pains shooting up and down her abdomen pleading for something more. But there is nothing.

Ever since the Pilgrim fathers and mothers "gathered together to ask the Lord's blessing," Americans have given thanks to God—especially on Thanksgiving Day—for the bounties and goodness of life in the United States. And, comparatively speaking, we *do* have so much. In a land boasting plenty, we express our gratitude to God for our country's many blessings.

But the three Thanksgiving scenarios I have shared with you—the Cain family, the Ortiz family, and Amusiri's family—prompt a crucial theological question. And the question is this: Why is there so much in America? Why are *we* blessed?

Is it because we Americans are morally superior to other people? It would hardly seem so! On a personal level, you and I know how far we fall short of being the kind of people God would have us be. We know too well the truth of Paul's declaration in Romans that "*all* have sinned and fall short of the glory of God" (3:23).

And on a national level, our political history reads like a composite scorecard of anything *but* minor misdemeanors. And our economic history reveals the greed of businesses and international corporations that promises that the more "stuff" you have, the happier you will be, and the more "toys" you have to play with, the more successfully you will be regarded.

No, America has not been blessed by God because we are more moral than other people.

Why are *we* blessed?

Is it because we work harder and are more energetic and industrious than everyone else in the world? In spite of the pervasive influence of the Protestant work ethic, this hardly seems the case. We *do* work hard and put in a lot of hours. But we have such technologies and conveniences to assist us in our work!

Mr. Ortiz leaves the house at 4:30 AM and works road construction for 14 hours until 6:30 PM. When he returns home, he immediately works in his little garden in back of the house until suppertime at 8:30. After he eats, he plays with his children until 9:00 or so and then goes to bed, so that he can start the whole routine all over again the next morning. And Mr. Ortiz works this hard for $500 a year.

No, I think that we may conclude that we are not blessed by God because we Americans work harder than other people in the world. Many work as hard, if not harder, and comparatively they have little or nothing to show for it.

Is it because we are spiritual Christians and other people are either not Christian or not so spiritual?

Rightly or wrongly, America has been called a "Christian" nation. In fact, certain religious folks constantly implore the country to return to its basic roots as a political entity founded on Christian principles.

Some people have even talked in terms of a "manifest destiny"—that is, that God has a special, spiritual stake in the well-being and progress of the United States of America. A few have even claimed divine endorsement for policies, characteristics, and decisions in the United States. Fewer still, have been so bold as to link confidently God's will for the world with the fulfillment of American desires and self-interest. There have been some who have even sanctioned our military engagements with other countries as "holy wars," campaigns that God especially endorses.

Is this why we are blessed? Do we Americans have a special "in" with God?

It would hardly seem so: In fact, the Bible is chock-full of correctives to this way of thinking. The prophet Isaiah reminded his fellow countrypersons that God was God of the whole earth, of *all* peoples (Isaiah 40:21-31; 45:21-22; 55:1-13; 66:1). Because of this, Israel never had God, but rather God had Israel. And that difference makes all the difference in the world.

We are to worship *God*, not the nation. To engage in nationalism is to succumb to idolatry—worshipping something less than God as if it *were* God!

Why are *we* blessed?

Maybe a passage from Genesis 12 in the Hebrew Bible points us in a direction which will begin to answer that persistent question. It may be that America is blessed *in order to bless others*. It may be that we have so much as a nation as a whole, so that we may share our national abundance with those who are needy—both abroad and at home.

Just as the Pilgrims called together their Native American neighbors to share a bountiful harvest, so we Americans must send out the word that the American table of plenty has room for those whose tables are meager or empty. I cannot think of any better way than this to understand God's promise to Abraham and to Abraham's religious descendants (i.e., you and me) that God will bless God's people and make them (us) a blessing to others (Genesis 12:2-3).

As we sit down on Thanksgiving Day, 400 people will starve in just one of the provinces of Amusiri's country in Africa. And that's in just one part of one nation in one continent. Over one million Africans will die from hunger between Thanksgiving morning and our singing the first verse of "Joy to the World" at Christmas.

As we sit down on Thanksgiving Day, many Latin Americans will make do with the meager morsels they have because they have no other choice. And they will watch some of their children grow weaker and weaker from malnutrition.

If we do not intend to share our American blessings, how can we conscientiously give God thanks at Thanksgiving? I believe that we cannot!

If we do not intend to examine our individual lives and the life of our communities in terms of what commitment to Christ as Lord and Savior means, how can we grab that food with gusto? I believe that we cannot!

If we do not intend to ask ourselves the personal and national question, "What can be done to be a blessing to people who suffer from poverty, poor health, malnutrition, and oppression?", how can we joke and laugh in the midst of American prosperity, ease, and national affluence? I believe that we cannot!

If we do not intend to scrutinize our own country's political and economic policies as a powerful boat of "haves" afloat in a sea of "have-nots," how can we comfortably ask for seconds of the pumpkin pie? I believe that we cannot!

For it is clear from Jesus' words in Matthew 25, that he identifies with the "least of these"—the hungry, the oppressed, the naked, the sick, the thirsty, and the stranger. In fact, in a mysterious and mystical way, he *is* one of them: "Whenever you do it to the one of the least of these, you do it also to me" (Matthew 25:40).

Unless we can respond to the presence of Jesus in the terrified eyes of the oppressed and in the exposed ribs of the hungry and in the dirty tattered clothing of the poor, how can we conscientiously give thanks to God at Thanksgiving? I believe that we cannot!

The Pilgrims *shared* their blessings. And what rejoicing there must have been in heaven and on earth!

Scripture for reflection: Genesis 12:1-3; Matthew 25:31-40

The Word Became *Flesh*!

Does matter matter? Is the physical world around us important? Are our bodies significant?

Voices from the past have said, "No." The philosopher Plato concluded that the world around us was not valuable. It changes, he observed, and change must involve imperfection and decay. For Plato, the unchanging—the *eternal*—was what solely mattered.

Since our souls were eternal, they were *important*, they were valuable, said Plato. Our bodies were changing, and they were of little importance, not ultimately valuable at all. Matter didn't matter.

The early Church Fathers agreed. The physical world was perishing. It was "a vale of tears and sorrows" anyway. It wasn't what really mattered. The status of one's soul before God was the only thing that was finally important.

Classical Christian theology's understanding of the spiritual life concurred. Our physical bodies were the source of temptation, sin, and all sorts of dangerous desires. The life of the spirit—the purity of our souls—could be hampered, harmed, corrupted, even forfeited, through its being dragged-down by the desires and deceits of the body and the physical world.

That's why the "higher" calling of celibacy—non-marriage and refraining from sexual intimacy—was so highly-valued and persistently-preferred in the life of the Church. For those who were too weak to resist the passions of the flesh and the unbridled physical temptations of the body, there were marriage, carnal knowledge, and procreation. But for those led to a higher life, a more righteous life, a more spiritual existence, there were celibacy and virginal abstinence.

Matter doesn't matter.

But "the Word became *flesh* and dwelt among us, full of grace and truth" (John 1:14). In Jesus of Nazareth—the baby born in Bethlehem—we see present the invisible and eternal God whose love and grace brought physical creation into being. In the baby born in a manger, in the man crucified on a cross outside the city walls of Jerusalem, we see present the invisible and eternal God whose love and grace brought reconciliation into the world. In a baby born of teenage parents who were engaged but not yet married, we see present the invisible and eternal God whose love and grace brought hope-for-a-better-day into being.

Matter matters. At least it matters to *God*! When it came time for God to manifest God's very nature, God used the means of becoming flesh, of being born in a physical form, like all babies before and like all babies since. When it came time for God to display God's very self, God chose the common and the mundane, the ordinary and the everyday. When it came time for God to communicate God's "Good News" (*Gospel*) to us, God elected to couch that News in physical form. Matter matters to God!

So the Word became *flesh*. And this divine Incarnation—this taking-on of matter—communicates at least three things to us:

First, our bodies are not to be taken lightly. What we do to them, what we do with them, is important in our Christian living. Our bodies can be the expression of anger and violence, or of patience and kindness. Our bodies can be the object of self-mortification and disrespect, or of appropriate appreciation and self-esteem.

Too many persons think negatively or badly of themselves because they don't have glamorous appearances and perfect bodies. Too many persons suffer low-esteem, deprecating self-images, and eating disorders.

But the Word became flesh and dwelt among us, full of grace and truth. And one meaning of this, one implication of the Incarnation, is that because God took on human form and became one of us, matter matters. Our bodies are not to be taken lightly. Our "bodies are the temples of the Holy Spirit," as the Apostle Paul put it in I Corinthians (6:19), and as such, they are special and sacred. And sacred things are to be appreciated, even treasured. As the Psalmist declares, "I praise you [God], for I am fearfully and wonderfully made" (Psalm 139:14). What we do *to* our bodies is important in our Christian living.

And what we do *with* our bodies is not to be taken lightly either. When we are loving to others—through kind words and kind deeds—we are conduits of divine love and grace. And when we are mean and nasty and unforgiving and vengeful, we are reflectors of what is sinful and wrong with life in the world. Living righteously before God, living the good life in our communities, is not a matter of only doing those things—like praying, going to church, singing Christian hymns and praise songs—that cultivate the life of the spirit alone, to the neglect of our physical selves. We cannot "live lives of sin from Monday mornings until Saturday nights" and then have our souls assured of their salvation on Sundays.

As the Letter to the Colossians admonishes,

> Clothe yourselves with compassion, kindness, humility, meekness and patience . . . [and] with love, which binds everything together in perfect harmony. (3:12, 14)

Our bodies are not to be taken lightly. What we do *to* them, what we do *with* them, is important in our Christian living.

Second, our human sexuality is something that is *good*, not something that is bad. Garrison Keillor, of "Prairie Home Companion" fame, tells this joke: An old woman was sitting in a rocking chair on her porch, petting her cat, "Alex." A magical fairy appears and says, "I'm here to give you three wishes." The old woman replies, "I wish I were 19 years old and beautiful again." Poof! She is. "Now I wish I had a million dollars and this old house was a mansion." Poof! Done. "And now, I wish that "Alex" was not a cat, but was the most handsome man in the whole world and was deeply in love with me." Poof! Suddenly she's in the arms of the best-looking man in the whole world. He kisses her and whispers, "Darling, aren't you sorry you had me neutered?"

Our human sexuality is something that is good, not something that is bad.

The proverbial "dirty joke" about sex is not "dirty" because sex is bad. It is dirty because sex is *good*. God gave us sexual desire, sexual responsiveness, and sexual pleasure that would permit us humans to enjoy sexual intimacy and communion.

Of course, we are to be sexually-*responsible* as well as sexually-*responsive*. But when sex celebrates an intellectual, emotional, and spiritual intimacy between two persons, it is elevated to the level of *agape* love—a self-giving, gracious-receiving kind of love . . . a *divine* kind of love. In the Jewish tradition, it is said that God smiles when two persons make love on *Shabbat*, the Sabbath day of the week. I think it can be argued in the Christian tradition that God smiles when two persons make love in a deeply-engaged, mutually-loving, powerfully-committed, multi-layered way *on any day of the week*!

The Word became flesh and dwelt among us. And so, our human sexuality is something that is good, not something that is bad. And things that are good, that are sacred, are to be taken good care of!

Third, because matter matters, we ought to be concerned about the degradation of the good earth which God created and placed in our care. When God made the world, God pronounced it "good". And when the world had fallen into sin and disrepair—since God loved the world—God came in human form to save it (John 3:16) and to repair it.

Can we humans, "made in God's image" (Genesis 1:26-27), try to do any *less*?

Acid rain is falling down, while garbage dumps are filling up. Global warming is increasing, while nonrenewable natural resources are decreasing. Species are becoming extinct, while human populations are burgeoning. The ozone is thinning, while pollution is thickening. Oil spills are oozing everywhere, while toxic waste is headed anywhere that will take it.

At the first Christmas, the Word became flesh—became incarnate, entered the world of matter, of neutrons, protons, and electrons, of quarks and quasars, of leptons and septons, of geology and chemistry, of biology and ecology—*and dwelt among us*, full of grace and truth. Matter matters. And since it matters to *God*, it must matter also to *us*:

> Our bodies are not to be taken lightly;
> Our human sexuality is something that is
> good, not something that is bad;
> We ought to be concerned about the
> environmental crisis which has
> beset God's creation, the earth
> that God has placed in our care.

The Word became *flesh* and dwelt among us, full of grace and truth. For God so *loved* the world, that God gave God's Son.

The Word became flesh . . . God loved. The Word became flesh God loved!

Scripture for reflection: John 1:1-5, 14

999 Patrons

For most of us, the Wise Men represent a regal, but mysterious presence: We sing at Christmas time, "We three kings of Orient are, bearing gifts, we traverse afar." But only the Gospel of Matthew mentions these three figures, and they burst on us immediately following the story of Jesus' birth. Coming most probably from what is modern-day Iran, their name—*magi*— suggests that they were likely either Persian astrologers or Zoroastrian priests. The text tells us that they honed-in to the guidance of a star, following it to a land foreign to them.

Their identities are unknown to us through the Bible, but Christian tradition has embellished the account by giving them the names "Casper," who brings the gift of gold, "Melchior," who brings the gift of frankincense, and "Balthazzar," who brings the gift of myrrh. Then, being warned in a dream not to let Herod the Great know of their success in locating the Bethlehem babe, they pulled a "fast one" on the King and skeedaddled back to Persia by another route. And that is the end of it. They disappeared just as suddenly and mysteriously as they came.

We never hear from the Wise Men again. We never hear *about* the magi again. But we're left with the lingering awareness that a "trinity of out-of-town foreigners"—*Gentiles*—journeyed to a small, Jewish town just a stone's throw from Jerusalem and there worshipped a tiny infant.

We do not know what impact this trek and this worship had on them. We do not know whether they gave up astrology (the science of their time) for Christology (the study of the identity of Jesus as the Christ); we have no way of proving that they were irreversibly converted from Zoroastrianism to Christianity and perhaps spread that new faith in their homeland among their people.

What we *do* know is that they worshipped Jesus and laid expensive gifts—gifts "fit for a King"—*at his feet*. But we'll never be sure whether they followed *in his footsteps*.

Henry David Thoreau, in his wonderfully-stirring work, "Civil Disobedience," wrote these words: "There are thousands who are *in opinion* opposed to slavery and war, who yet do nothing to put an end to them. There are 999 *patrons of virtue* to every virtuous person."

Many persons say they *think* something is a good idea or they *theoretically support* a high idea or they *consider* a certain cause to be noble. It is quite another thing, Thoreau implies, to put that good idea *into practice* or to *live-out* a high ideal or to *take-up* a noble cause.

The magi worshipped at Jesus' feet; but did they follow in his footsteps? Were they simply *patrons of virtue*, or did they become virtuous themselves? Or to put it another way, did they merely "talk the walk," or did they also "walk the talk"?

The Letter of James implores us to be "hearers and doers of the Word." Hearing about Jesus, without deciding *for* Jesus, doesn't cut it. Knowing how Jesus wants you to live, and *not* living it, isn't what it's all about! You must hear the Word of God in your life and then *respond* to it.

How many of us know persons (maybe even *ourselves* at times!) who proclaim, "being good—I'm for *that*" or "living the Christ-centered life—that sounds *great*," or "Jesus—what a 'neat guy,'" yet never invite Jesus into their hearts and into their lives and strive to keep him there?

Devotion without transformation is faith without works.

That same Letter of James that admonishes us to "*do* the Word as well as *hear* it," is the same letter which warns us that "faith without works is dead." If you truly worship Jesus, then your life is forever changed. "By our deeds, other persons shall know of our faith."

When I was beginning my career, I met a scientist whose name I'll call "Mark." Mark was a thoroughgoing atheist, a person for whom truth was equivalent only to what could be dissected in a laboratory or observed under an electron microscope. But Mark suddenly came down with a disease and became quite ill. Word also spread around the campus that he felt quite isolated and lonely. I decided to visit him.

When I arrived at his house where he was recovering, I carefully stood at a distance across the room—after all, he had an infectious disease, and he was an atheist to boot! But then Mark asked, "What are you doing here, Cliff? Nobody else has come. Why, you?" I replied that I believed that God loved him, and I did, too. I told him that I thought that God was present with him in this tough time, and that I wanted to be there, too, in order to be supportive.

Two years later, Mark joined a local church in the community. He asked me to be his sponsor for membership. Of course, I agreed. It remains one of the most special and memorable moments in my life.

"What are you *doing* here?" he had asked. What are you *doing*? It is clear that we can share the *words* that the Jesus at whose feet we worship loves the world and wants the world to be saved. Or, we can also *participate* with Jesus in healing and saving the world by following in his footsteps.

Over seventy years ago, the great Hindu holy man, Mohandas K. Gandhi, was asked how he reacted to persons' adoration and adulation of him. This renowned person of nonviolence, love, and tolerance answered honestly, "I wish persons would not so much kiss my feet as follow in my footsteps!"

Each year, our minds and communal memory—like the "star in the East"—take us back again nearly 2,000 years to a humble stable setting in a small town in a faraway place. And as presents are bought and wrapped, cookies are baked, carols are sung, trees are decorated, and holiday travel is arranged, we make the journey back in time to Bethlehem where we lay our gifts of nostalgia, familiarity, and warm fuzzies at the feet of Jesus.

But what's important, of course, is *this*: Do we plan, in the New Year, to follow in his footsteps? Let's be honest: We find it easier (and more comfortable and more convenient) to accept Jesus as "Savior" than to make him our "Lord." But Jesus turns to us, and says, "Then let me rule your life. Let me run your thoughts. Let me inform your feelings. Let me direct your actions. Let me adjust your attitudes. Let me be the Lord of your lives as well as the Savior of your souls . . . For, after all, there are 999 *patrons* of virtue to every virtuous person."

The late and great African-American preacher and pastor, Howard Thurmond, once penned these words:

> When the song of the angels is still,
> When the star in the sky is gone,
> When the kings and princes are home,
> When the shepherds are back with their sheep,
> The work of Christmas begins:
> To find the lost,
> To heal the broken,
> To feed the hungry,
> To release the prisoner,
> To rebuild the nations,
> To bring peace among people,
> To make music in the heart.

A User-friendly Universe?

The magi came and went. Each Christmas comes and goes. We don't know whether the three Wise Men followed in Jesus' footsteps as well as worshipped at his feet.

But we *do* know about **us**! So let today be the beginning of a new intention; let this day be the time for a renewed dedication; let this present moment be one of committed *discipleship*.

For we want to be true and transformed followers of Jesus Christ. We don't want to settle for being just 999 *patrons* of virtue!

Scripture for reflection: Matthew 2:1-12; James 1:19-27, 2:14-18, 26; Luke 4:16-21

The Essence of Christianity

Over fifty years ago, one of the most famous theologians in the world made his first visit to the United States. Swiss by birth, he had exploded onto the theological scene just after the conclusion of World War I with a commentary on Paul's Letter to the Romans. A decade-and-a- half later, he had gotten himself into political trouble while teaching at a university in Germany by challenging the ideology of the Nazis and prophetically protesting the elevation of Adolf Hitler as the New Messiah. He then refused to take the required, patriotic loyalty oath to Hitler and was subsequently dismissed from his post. Knowing that his life might be in jeopardy, he beat a hasty retreat to his native Switzerland to an endowed chair created for him at the University of Basel. But, of course, naturally, geographical distance could not shut him up, and he continued to shout-out that only God is worthy of worship, never a nation itself, and certainly not its leader.

Not much of a world traveler, he contented himself with life centered in Basel—teaching his classes, meeting with his students in a café across the street from his home, smoking his pipe, reading detective stories, writing pages and pages and pages of theology (in very long German sentences!), and listening to the music of Mozart. He once remarked that if the angels were permitted to indicate their favorite composer, they would unquestionably gush forth in an unrestrained chorus, "Mozart."

Finally, nearly 20 years after the end of World War II and the defeat of Hitler and Nazism, several prestigious American universities and seminaries were able to persuade this theologian to leave the Alps and Switzerland and his students behind for a brief time and visit the United States and present some lectures. This would be his only trip to America. The theologian's name is Karl Barth.

After Karl Barth's lecture at Union Theological Seminary in Richmond, Virginia, a group of students and faculty gathered with the eminent theologian for an informal discussion. One of the seminarians asked Professor Barth this question: "What in your judgment is the essence of the Christian faith?"

Barth did not immediately answer, but paused for a few moments. No doubt everyone assembled in the room was waiting for some great, heavy theological response, perhaps very lengthy as well. The silence was deafening, the anticipation weighty. Finally, Karl Barth replied, "I think I can summarize it in very few words. This is my understanding of the essence of the Christian faith—'Jesus loves me, this I know, for the Bible tells me so. Little ones to him belong; they are weak, but he is strong. Yes, Jesus loves me, yes, Jesus loves me; yes, Jesus loves me, the Bible tells me so.'"

What is the essence of Christianity?—Jesus loves me.

One of the earliest affirmations of the Christian tradition is that God is love. That is, the basic nature of God, the primary characteristic of transcendent divinity, is love.

Of course, we begin to understand divine love through our observation of human love. We witness parents, young people, church people, and individual Christians caring about others, putting others first, and serving one another. We see tenderness, sympathy, empathy, and devotion. We see active goodwill wanting positive things to happen for other people.

These experiences give us some sense of how God is, how God loves. Later, perhaps, we come to see that it is God's love which actually lies behind human love—that *we* are able to love because God loves us first. The First Letter of John (4:19) tells us that God so fills us with God's love that it overflows to other people—much the same way that a plugged sink or an unattended bathtub will overflow and saturate everything around it if we forget to turn the water off or leave it on for just a minute or so too long. As the British writer, A.E. Brooke, put it over a hundred years ago, "Human love is a reflection of something in the divine nature itself."

But at least initially it would seem, we come to understand God's love by extrapolating from expressions in our everyday lives of human love.

As we develop and mature as human beings, as we develop and mature as Christians, we find the Bible filling-in the outline of this basic understanding of love with mosaic-like pieces involving verses or stories. We learn that "God so loved, that God sacrificially gave," that "a person has no greater love than this, that she/he would lay down her/his life for a friend," that "God is love and that whoever abides in love, abides in God."

We also learn about the story of Jesus, who threw aside a safe profession as a carpenter and forsook personal security way-up north in the Galilee far from the political madness in Jerusalem, in order to follow the mission which God had laid on him, in order to follow the mission for which God had become incarnate in him.

One of the earliest American folk hymns is entitled, "What Wondrous Love Is This?," and the first verse contains these lines:

> What wondrous love is this, oh
> my soul, oh my soul?:
> What wondrous love is this, oh my soul!
> What wondrous love is this, that
> caused the Lord of bliss,
> To bear the heavy cross for my soul, for my soul?
> To bear the heavy cross for my soul!

And so, we as Christians have grown to see that when we encounter the loving person of Jesus, when we come to know the loving deeds of Jesus, when we choose to relate to the living Christ who loves us today, we are standing face-to-face with a *God* who loves us.

"Jesus loves me, this I know, for the Bible tells me so." Could there be any better theological answer to the question, "What is the essence of Christianity?"? There may be longer answers, there may be weightier answers, there may be more complicated answers. But I would suggest that there is no more profound answer than Karl Barth's—"Jesus loves me."

The late Robert M. Grant was a professor of early Christianity and New Testament at the University of Chicago. In a book entitled, *Gods and the One God*, Professor Grant points out that our Christian faith has made some very important contributions to the world's theological understanding. One of those contributions is this: The one, true God who is, *loves* us!

Prior to Christianity (and, of course, to Judaism as well), the predominant belief in the world was that there were many gods, not just one. In fact, polytheism—the assertion that there are numerous gods—has a much longer history than monotheism.

The corollary belief that often accompanied the notion of polytheism was that these many gods were both fickle and apathetic. That is, they could change their minds and dispositions in an instant, and they really didn't care much about what happened to persons in the world. *Psychology Today* would say that these gods 'exhibited pronounced and constant mood swings and were unmoved by human cries of distress directed to them.'

As a result, the worship of such fickle and apathetic gods consisted mainly and chiefly of sacrifices. Grains, animals, even human beings, were sacrificed in order to gain (hopefully) the goodwill of the gods. Perhaps by parting with something valued, one could entice the gods to do something nice. Perhaps.

Our Christian notion of God, our "faith picture" of the way God is, is quite different. We gather to worship a God who loves us, a God who doesn't have to be won-over to our side. We worship a God who so loved us and everyone else in the world that this God made the supreme sacrifice for *us*—the gift of God's Son, Jesus Christ.

The essence of Christianity—the affirmation that Jesus loves us—celebrates that God is already "on our side"—not sanctioning all that we do (for some of our actions are certainly sinful), but faithfully remaining favorable to our best interests and constantly caring about our discomforts and problems. Christian worship is predicated on that fact; Christian worship does not try to produce that fact. God loves you; Jesus loves you. We gather for worship in response to this; we don't come to a worship service to try to cause this to happen.

To put this yet another way, we engage in worship because God *already* loves us. We don't worship God to try to *get* God to love us.

This, then, is the essence of Christianity—

> Jesus loves me, this I know. For the Bible tells me so. Little ones to him belong. They are weak, but he is strong. Yes, Jesus loves me; yes, Jesus loves me; yes, Jesus loves me, the Bible tells me so.

Scripture for reflection: Psalm 138; I John 4:7-12

Christ and Culture

When the Israelites moved into Canaan, the land was not empty. There were several peoples situated there, one of the chief groups being the Canaanites.

The Bible gives us a picture of the Canaanites through "theological" lenses: That is, the Canaanites are the "bad" guys, the Israelites are the "good" guys, and the battles between these two, opposing forces for possession of the "land of milk and honey" is cast in theological images—God fights on the side of the Israelites (when they are faithful and keep the covenant) against the Canaanites.

The Canaanites, to be sure, were not atheists. They may have been "pagan"—that is, they did not practice the Jewish religion—but they were not unbelievers. Instead, they believed in a number of gods, two keys ones being Baal and Ashtart. These two gods were responsible for soil fertility, the amount of rain that fell, and the abundance of the harvest. The Canaanites prayed to these two gods, built altars to them, and made sacrificial offerings to them.

When the Israelites moved into the Promised Land, the land of Canaan, they ceased being nomads who tended flocks of sheep and who were always on the move. Now, after 40 years of wandering in the Sinai desert, they settled down and became farmers.

Canaanite culture was attractive to the Israelites, not only because of its relative sophistication regarding metallurgy and weapons production, but also because the Israelite-farmers liked the idea of a god like Baal who took care of the farm and granted a good crop. But there was yet another attraction here: The way in which rainfall and an abundant harvest were guaranteed was for Baal, the male Canaanite god, and Ashtart, the female Canaanite god, to have intercourse. This creativity (their intimacy), in turn, produced the creativity of the soil.

Now you don't have to guess very hard how one might engage in the worship of these two gods whose intercourse ensured a good year in farming. Right: Humans had intercourse during worship as a way of imitating the two gods.

So, I think you can see that this was an additional attraction for Israelites toward Canaanite culture and Canaanite religion! And throughout the Israelites' sojourn in the land of Canaan, they flirted with Baal, this most attractive aspect of Canaanite culture.

It was the worship of the god Baal which the prophet Elijah sought to undo in the contest on Mt. Carmel. How moving the scripture passage in I Kings 18 is of that story, and how powerful-looking is the statue of Elijah which sits on the top of Mt. Carmel in Israel today to remind the viewer of the victory of the Lord over Baal and the vindication of Elijah over the 450 prophets of Baal.

Throughout the centuries, faith and culture have had a most interesting relationship. Sometimes faith has rejected culture altogether, regarding it as being totally hostile to religion. Sometimes faith has affirmed culture, finding in it some things which contributed in helpful and healthy ways to religion. Other times faith has criticized culture but then worked to change it, acknowledging some positive potential to be found there.

Around three thousand years after Elijah and the prophets of Baal, theologian H. Richard Niebuhr wrote a book entitled *Christ and Culture*, which outlined a number of ways in which Christian faith and human culture have related and could relate. Three of them line-up with what I shared in the previous paragraph: "Christ against culture" points to a rejection of culture by faith. "Christianity and Culture" affirms culture. And "Christ over culture" describes the transformation of culture by faith.

A User-friendly Universe?

In the New Testament, Paul in his letter to the church at Rome advises us not to conform ourselves to the world, but to be transformed by the renewing of our minds so that we can discover what is good and acceptable and perfect (12:2). Paul seems here to be suggesting that worldly standards are not what we should accept nor are they that by which we ought to make judgments: For example, the world says look out for yourself only, for if you don't, no one else will! Our faith says to be concerned about others and to share. The world says pay back evil for evil. Our faith says to overcome evil with good.

Paul seems to be advocating the "Christ transforming culture" model: Our faith ought to criticize those things around us in society which are not what they ought to be or are not in-line with the values of our Christian tradition.

So what are some of these things that must be criticized and changed? What are some of the "Baals" and "Ashtarts" in our American culture?

I think especially of three (although the total number certainly exceeds these three): The first I would call "rugged individualism." Rugged individualism in America undoubtedly originated with the pioneer spirit of taming the frontier. In those times, a person lived by his own effort and survived on sheer perseverance and guts. Although that person depended somewhat on others in events such as barn-raisings, there was a sense of independence and self-reliance.

This attitude has survived to today. For there is a sense that the strong, bright, in-control person simply does not need other persons. He/she can do it alone!

However, a number of writers and researchers have pointed out the growing sense among persons in contemporary American society that there is great loneliness and a feeling of being separated from others. Sociologist Robert Bellah reveals through his studies that what persons desire most of all is community—that is, a sense of relationship with, and an acknowledgement of inevitable interdependence on, other persons.

The Christian faith also recognizes theologically what Bellah has recognized sociologically: We need people more than we would ever assume. That's why Jesus and Paul talk so much about the proper way to maintain relationships. Jesus tells us in Matthew 22 that loving God and loving our neighbor summarize the Law, the Jewish *Torah*. (verses 36-40). And Paul says in Romans 12 that we are actually "members one of another" and that we ought to "love one another with mutual affection," "honor" one another, exhibit "patience," help others in their needs, and even "extend hospitality to strangers" (verses 5, 9-13).

So the first "Baal" that must be criticized and transformed in our American culture is that of "rugged individualism."

The second "Baal" which faith must call into question and attempt to change is a regard for violence as the preferred way for solving problems. Television constantly airs shows with cops and private investigators and other characters who regularly punch-up (and punch-out) people in the line-of-duty. Children's toys glorify both violence and war.

Further, and less lethally, our society regards sports figures as heroes, paying them ludicrous salaries, and especially in regard to football, making "delivering a hard tackle or a devastating block" very macho and very male. Boxing and mixed martial arts cage fighting involve both men and women, occupying prime time spots and regularly and readily available via pay-per-view. And even the fake wrestling on tv—more "show" than "real," more "theatre" than "sport"—has attracted an incredibly large and faithful following.

We are a violent society. One past political figure confessed that "violence is as American as apple pie." And yet, the Christian faith speaks in ways such as "forgive seventy times seven," "thou shalt not kill," "blessed are the peacemakers," and "love your enemies."

The second "Baal" which the Christian faith must address is the American penchant for using violence as the valued, preferred, and wide-spread way of solving problems.

The third "Baal" is consumerism and materialism. We are a society obsessed with the accumulation of "things." The universally-recognized battle cry is "*Shop 'Til You Drop!*"

Recently, I was speaking to a student on our campus who had just gone through the difficult emotional turbulence of the break-up of a relationship. I asked the person how that person had dealt with the severing of that very special "love connection." The person answered without blinking an eye, "I went on a spending spree at the Mall."

The advertisements on television and in newspapers and magazines are predicated on the myth that buying is an antidote to pain, suffering, boredom, and meaninglessness. Surrounded by our acquisitions, we live lives filled with "stuff." We wrongly think that, insulated by such "purchased layers" (like the Michelin tire man), we will be safe and happy.

By contrast, the Christian faith says that a happy, meaningful life involves giving, not getting; sharing, not hoarding; and giving away, not keeping. French existentialist thinker and writer Jean-Paul Sartre, though certainly no Christian, said a very Christian-like thing when he remarked, "When something physical means a lot to me, I give it away; I don't want that kind of thing to have power over me."

Our Christian faith declares that what's really important is not material possessions, but relationships; not the quantity of things you have accumulated, but the quality of persons you love and care about. Faith stresses that it is not what you *have* that counts, but rather what you *are*—not "cash," but "character."

Three "Baals" (at least!) confront us in our culture, beckoning us to worship them, to elevate them to our top priority position:

> *Rugged Individualism*, which says, "I don't need you,
> I can make do all by myself. So leave me alone and
> I'll do the same to you."

> *Violence* as the preferred, prevalent way to solve problems—"do unto others," and then quickly get out of there!
>
> And an *Acquisitive Consumerism* which advises, "Be happy—buy something!" and promises that, as the bumper sticker reads, "The person who dies with the most toys, wins!"

But our faith responds, challenging these "Baals" and challenging *us*—

> You shall have no other gods before the God and Father of our Lord Jesus Christ. (Exodus 20)
>
> You shall love the Lord your God with all your heart, and with all your soul, and with all your mind . . . And you shall love your neighbor as yourself. (Matthew 22)
>
> So, do not conform yourself to the world but be transformed by the renewing of your mind, so that you can discover what is good and acceptable and perfect. (Romans 12)

Scripture for reflection: I Kings 18:20-39; Romans 12:1-13

What Is Faith?

Is Christianity a creed to be believed? Is it a life to be lived? Is it a means of getting a passport into heaven? Is it a cheap way of acquiring fire insurance against hell?

One person will say that what you *believe* is what counts. Another will advise you, I don't care what you believe, it's how you *live* your life that's most important. Yet another will contend that the chief thing is to be "saved," that is, to ensure that you are going to heaven and are not destined for hell.

Are all of these answers right, or wrong? Are they *entirely* wrong? Surely *not*. But surely also, none of them is big enough, exhaustive enough, or comprehensive enough, to fully encompass the "right" answer.

A.M. Hunter, professor *emeritus* at the University of Aberdeen in Scotland, answered the question, "What is Christianity?" by responding, "*Faith* is the essential piece of [the Christian] religion."

But what does "faith" mean? What is faith? Faith is one of those words, like "love," that means so many different things.

Sometimes we confuse "faith" with "belief." So when we say, "I have faith in God," we mean that we believe in God. But "belief" suggests an intellectual act, a mental assent to a proposition or a creedal statement or an assertion about reality.

Beliefs are immensely important. Nevertheless, when a Christian says, "I believe," that person means more than intellectual assent to a formula of words, however majestic and profound they may be.

Of course, it is easier to say what faith is not, than to say what faith is. Faith is certainly not what a person once remarked to me: "Faith is believin' what you know ain't so."

Faith is not what Alice in *Alice in Wonderland* was told. When Alice did not believe some preposterous thing, she was told to shut her eyes, take a deep breath, and try again!

If I believe what some persons are reported to believe—that drinking V-8 juice will cause a third set of teeth to grow, that eating oysters will make someone a sexual superman (or superwoman), or that eating the crusts of toasted bread will put hair on young boys' chests—that is not faith, it is superstition.

To be sure, faith is a conviction that certain propositions or affirmations are true—God is the Creator of the universe, Jesus is the Christ, earthly existence is not all there is, you can find your life only by losing it in the service of others. But faith is also more than this.

Perhaps a good working definition of faith is "entrusting yourself to another." This is what is meant in the traditional language of the marriage ceremony, where both the bride and the groom end their vows to each other by saying, "And thereto I plight thee my troth." "Troth" is the old word for faith.

In the marriage vows, the groom and the bride each promise to the other, "I pledge you my faith, my loyalty. I love you, and therefore I trust you with my life and well-being."

One day a hiker ventured dangerously close to the edge of a ravine. Losing his balance, he tumbled over the side. Fortunately, there was a thin, small shrub growing about 30 feet below, and the young man grabbed it as he slid by, and held-on for dear life. Looking down, he saw the floor of the canyon 200 feet below. Looking up, he saw only blue sky. Desperately he shouted, "Is anybody up there?" A discernible voice replied, "I, the Lord your God, am up here."

"Oh, help me, help me, I beg you, help me," the man pleaded. "Do you have faith in me, do you trust me?" came back the response. "Yes, oh, yes, definitely, to be sure, I have faith in you, I trust you," proclaimed the hiker. God then said, "If so, if you trust me, if you have faith in me, then let go your hand."

The man looked down, the man look over at his weak grip on the shrub, and then he looked up to the blue sky again. So he shouted as loudly as he could, "Is there anybody *else* up there?"

What is faith? Faith is trusting in God; faith is entrusting one's life to the Divine.

Christian faith is trusting one's self to the God made known in Jesus Christ. What we Christians know about God we know through Jesus. And what we know through Jesus is that God loves us, cares for us, helps us, and wants what's best for us. Seminary theology professor *emeritus* Dan Migliore, puts it this way: "Christian faith is basically trust in the freely gracious and loving God made known in Jesus Christ."

When my son, Zachary, was very little, I wanted him to learn how to swim. I remember distinctly his standing close-by the side of the pool, occasionally bravely dipping his big toe into the water. I was standing out in the 3 foot-4 foot section of the water and I called to him, "Zach, jump in. I'll catch you. Don't worry; trust me; I won't let anything bad happen to you."

And Zachary would summon forth enough courage to stand on his tippy-toes right at the pool's edge, but he was reticent (literally) "to take the plunge." So I encouraged him, "Zach, it'll be okay. Zach you can do this. Zach, you can trust your daddy."

Finally, Zach was willing to place enough faith in my reliability, good intentions, love, and care, that he jumped in. Then, having taken the risk, he kept getting-out and jumping-in, until I was not only weary, but also wondering about the wisdom in getting him used to the water in the first place!

The point is obvious: Zachary had to put trust in another person, he had to have faith that I was trustworthy and that I had his best interests at heart.

And that is what *we* must do: We must have enough trust in God, enough faith that God is trustworthy and has our best interests at heart that we are willing to commit ourselves to the relationship. Jesus encourages us, "Trust in God always, trust also in me" (John 14:1).

Consider *Alice in Wonderland* again: When Alice asked the Dodo, "What is a Caucus race?," she got the reply, "The best way to *explain* it is to *do* it." And, do it they did.

This is what Hebrews 11 is saying to us. That chapter begins with a statement which answers our persistent question, "What is faith?" Verse 1 says that "faith is the assurance of things hoped for, the conviction of things not seen." Then the writer shows us examples of faith in action: We are given a list of famous Jewish figures actually living-out their faith:

> Abel through faith came up with the gift which would meet God's approval; Noah faithfully built an ark in the face of impending doom and thereby gave the world a future; Abraham by faith ventured forth from the known to the unknown; Moses because of his faith refused to be regarded as Pharaoh's daughter's son and instead stood with his people and suffered ill-treatment with them; the people of Israel by faith passed through the Red Sea as if it were dry land and thereby escaped Egyptian pursuit and a return to slavery; Jesus, because of his faith, declared to God in the Garden of Gethsemane, "Not *my* will, but *yours* be done."

You and I know other persons—probably, undoubtedly, less well-known and not famous at all—who put their faith (their "assurance of things hoped for," their "conviction of things not seen") to work in their lives in the world. Perhaps it's a teacher or a coach or a neighbor or a person at church or a friend or an athlete or a pastor or a local professional you know who lives by trusting in God. The Letter to

A User-friendly Universe?

the Hebrews seems to shout out to us, "Look at persons around you who are living by faith in God!"

What is faith? "Faith" is *trust*. It is trusting in the good, gracious, and giving God who loved us so much that it involved self sacrifice.

What is faith? "Faith" is entrusting God with your life and your *well-being*.

What is faith? "Faith" is trusting our lives to the God *made known in Jesus Christ*.

What is faith? "Faith" is *the assurance of things hoped for, the conviction of things not seen*.

What is faith? "Faith" is a verb; it is a commitment; it is something that we *do*.

Scripture for reflection: Genesis 12:1-9; Hebrews 11:1-12

Fools, for Christ's Sake!

The greatest Christian, religious thinker of the thirteenth century was St. Thomas Aquinas. He was a monk who lived in an Italian monastery. He was also very gullible. There is a story—perhaps apocryphal—about St. Thomas which goes like this: The other monks at the monastery, knowing that Thomas was quite gullible, implored him to come to the window and look out and see a flying cow. Thomas complied, and when his gaze beheld no "elevated bovine," the other monks broke into uncontrollable laughter and teased him, saying, "Thomas, we really pulled one over on you. You're so gullible. You're such a fool!"

Thomas's response reportedly was the following words: "My brothers, I would think that a cow would fly rather than a monk would lie!"

There was *no* laughter in response to my friend, "Bill". Bill had a deep, deep crush on a young woman named "Laura." Bill was a shy person with a big heart and a generous wallet. His big heart made him vulnerable, and sometimes people took advantage of him. Bill showered Laura with all kinds of presents and took her to fancy restaurants, expensive concerts, and other places.

Bill misread Laura's feelings for him. She helped him misread her feelings for him! Bill thought she was genuinely interested in him. He even hoped that she loved him. So, imagine his surprise when he handed her a very expensive engagement ring and asked her to marry him: She tossed the ring back, and shouted to him, "You *fool*! You stupid, imbecilic jerk. I was only *using* you!"

The ambulance arrived at Bill's apartment not long after he had taken the pills. The driver and attendants raced him to the closest hospital. They pumped his stomach. He was in intensive care, then was moved to a regular hospital room. I was there when he regained consciousness. His first words to me were, "Why did they save my life? I am such a *fool*!"

It was *true* that he had acted foolishly in regard to Laura. She did use him, but he allowed her to do so. He had been a *fool;* he had not used his common sense; he had not used proper judgment; he was not sensible; he had been a simpleton.

A fool. No one likes to be a fool, for Christ's sake! There is something that recoils inside us when we think we may have been acting stupidly or may not have seen the truth or may have been taken advantage-of by someone.

But Paul, in his first letter to the Christian church at Corinth, Greece, says that *we* are "fools for Christ's sake" (4:10a). Paul says that you and I are *fools*! And earlier in his letter, Paul says that we Christians believe in Christ crucified, a stumbling-block to Jews and foolishness to Greeks (1:23).

To the pious first-century Jew, the claims about Jesus were regarded as sheer folly. To them, it was unthinkable that the Jesus of Nazareth who had been arrested, tried, sentenced, beaten, and crucified could be God's chosen one, the *Meshiach*, the "Messiah." To Jewish ears, the words "suffering Messiah" were an absolute contradiction in terms. For Jews, the Messiah was to be a victor, not the victim; heroic, not helpless; a winner, not a loser. For Jews, the fact of the crucifixion did not prove that Jesus was the expected One, it *disproved* it. Jewish folks during Jesus' time even pointed to sacred Scripture, the Torah, and a passage in Deuteronomy—"He that is hanged on a tree is cursed by God" (21:23). For Jews, the cross was an insurmountable barrier to belief in Jesus. To believe in Jesus as the Christ on that basis was complete foolishness!

Also, to the cultured Greek, the story of Jesus and claims about him were regarded as sheer folly. To Greeks, it was unthinkable that God could suffer. For the Greeks, the chief characteristic of God was *apatheia*, "apathy". To the Greeks, apathy meant more than mere indifference. It meant the total inability to feel. So the Greeks argued that if God felt joy or was influenced, then this God had lost his greatness and was not truly "God."

Therefore, God must be totally incapable of all feelings, so that no one or no thing may ever affect God. For the Greeks of the time, a God who suffered on the cross in the form of his only Son would be a contradiction in terms.

There is even more to it than this: The Greek thinker Plutarch said that it was in *insult* to God to describe God as involved in human affairs. God was utterly detached from the world and separate from human life in the world, transcendent to the comings-and-goings in the world. The idea of an *incarnation*, of God becoming human, of God assuming the form of a flesh-and-blood person, of God entering the world of human behavior and relationships, was *revolting* to the Greek mind. The "Word becoming flesh and dwelling among us" was a total intellectual impossibility for the Greeks.

So, the story and claims about Jesus were *foolishness* to *Jews* and *Gentiles* alike. That is, the story of Jesus was unacceptable to the cultural, philosophical, and religious mindset of that time. The story did not make sense; it was an affront to common sense. Popular wisdom said that these Christians were *fools*!

Now before we view the "foolishness of Christianity" as only a primitive problem in the early years of the emerging Christian movement, let us examine the contemporary situation in our own society.

Our society is one which has been permeated by the scientific method. That is, only that which is capable of being demonstrated in a laboratory or verified through careful observation is true. "Truth" comes from empirical proof. The statement, "Na+Cl=NaCl," or the statement, "There is a physical force called 'gravity'," is viewed as meaningful because we can test whether or not it is true.

The statement, "There is a God", however, is viewed as meaningless because we *cannot* test whether or not it is true. According to this way of thinking, religious statements are therefore statements for fools to hold as "true." You are a fool for believing in something which cannot be scientifically verified.

Our society is also one which has become incredibly pragmatic. That is, the good is what *works*. Our society says that the symbolic vision in the prophetic book of Isaiah of the lion lying down with the lamb, the child playing over the hole of the snake, swords being beaten into plowshares and spears into pruning hooks, does not make sense in a world which is plagued by terrorism, violence, killing, and war. Our society embraces a stark realism that pushes any idealism out of the picture. Our society defensively envisions the glass as half-empty rather than as half-full.

Therefore, the "good" is not to be seen in thinking of others, but in thinking only of yourself. After all, "If *you* don't look out for No. 1, who else is going to?" Our good is not to be found in forgiving our enemies and blessing those who persecute us, and turning the other cheek, and going the extra mile, and being the Good Samaritan who helps Third World countries to their feet. Rather, our good is to be found in intimidating our enemies and seeking revenge on those who persecute us, going the extra mile only if we can get some advantage from it, and keeping developing countries in their poverty and dependence so that we can continue to exploit them for our economic benefit.

Our society says that to think otherwise is to be naïve, stupid, a Pollyanna, a fuzzy-headed utopian, a *fool*. Our society makes fun of us Christians: "Quit being such fools, for Christ's sake!"

Is our local life vastly different? What place is there for Christian humility ("In humility count others better than yourselves") when we have to "sell ourselves" every day—whether in competition in the job market or in athletics or in the classroom, or in gaining social status or dating popularity, or in showing our colleagues and our supervisors and bosses "what we're made of"?

What place is there for Christian gentleness ("Blessed are the meek") when the aggressors and those driven by blind ambition are the ones who seem to get ahead, and when we are taught by the example of others that we can win only if someone else loses?

The popular wisdom of American culture would say that there is *no place* for such ideas, values, and virtues. And, only a *fool* would pursue them! "You Christians are all a bunch of fools, for Christ's sake!"

Holding Christian beliefs and values turns popular wisdom "upside down." To opt for, and make incarnate in our lives, humanity, gentleness, and kindness is to act in very "foolish" ways.

Of course, that's true only if we are informed by what appears to be wise, what seems to be true, and what is apparently the case.

The Apostle Paul says that God has made foolish the wisdom of the world. That suggests that our Christian faith has to do with the breaking-in of a revelation which tells us that what's *really* real, what's *finally* authentic, what's *ultimately* genuine, is different from what our society, what our culture, and indeed at times even what our local community, tell us.

God turns the wisdom of the world upside down! And God replaces it with the wisdom which says there's something truer, there's something better, there's something higher.

The world does not understand. Our society does not understand. Our community sometimes does not understand. But we Christians have perceived a truth, we have discerned a presence, we have communed with a risen Lord, which enables us to see things not as they *appear* to be, but as they *really* are. Jesus said, "I am the way, the *truth*, and the life." Through him, in him, and with him, we learn the wisdom that is *never* made foolish.

When we are told that using people is the only way to relate, we have wisdom that says differently.

When we are told that getting intoxicated or getting angry or grabbing the latest drug is the best way to handle our problems, our stressors, and our specific situation, we know differently.

When we are told that sex is no more special than a handshake, we know this is degrading of a good gift from a good Creator.

When we are told that seeking to retaliate is the only way to stand up for ourselves, we know another way.

When men are told that women are simply decorative playthings, we know that this is not what God had in mind in creating men and women "in the image of God."

When we are told that our faith is silly or stupid and our belief in God is a delusion or an "infantile projection," we are assured through our experience, through the Bible, through Jesus, and through that same faith, that there is a God who exists, who loves us, and who works for good in the world.

When we are told that only the "best" or the most "popular" count for anything and that therefore those people are the only *acceptable* ones, we know of a God who accepts everyone as God's children.

We are "fools for Christ's sake." But we are not "*fools*, for Christ's sake!" We are "fools for *Christ's* sake!"

Scripture for reflection: I Corinthians 1:18-31

Guilty

The television screen is black and white. The scene is a courtroom. The prosecuting attorney is Hamilton Berger. The defense attorney is the irrepressible Perry Manson. The defendant is accused of the murder of her overbearing, abusive, philandering husband. Is she guilty or is she innocent?

Witnesses are summoned by the court to give testimony. The prosecution calls its witnesses—persons who are able to contribute experiences, observations, and recognitions that will prove that the defendant did indeed commit the crime, that she is guilty as charged.

The defense also has its witnesses—persons who can counter the testimony of those whom the prosecution has summoned.

The judge ensures that the trial will proceed according to the letter and spirit of the law. The judge oversees the administration of justice and will render the sentencing of the defendant if found guilty, or declare the defendant cleared of all charges if found innocent.

The jury will weigh the evidence presented by both the prosecution and the defense. Will there be sufficient evidence to convict the defendant or will there not? The burden of proof lies on charges against the defendant which may be borne-out by the evidence presented.

Of course, in the television series, "Perry Manson," poor Mr. Berger seems always to lose. I watched the series as a little boy, and now I am seeing the series again on late-night television, so I feel confident in saying that Mr. Berger never wins against Perry

Mason. In fact, Hamilton Berger exudes some sort of masochism, always being willing to show up in the courtroom knowing that he has never won in the past (and will lose again in tonight's episode).

But, episode after episode after episode, the premise remains the same: Did the defendant do it or not? Can enough convicting evidence be marshalled to prove the defendant's guilt?

Susan B. Anthony was a major figure in the women's movement. My veterinarian daughter, Rachel, finds it incredulous that women did not have the right to vote until 1920 and the Nineteen Amendment to the Constitution! Susan B. Anthony found it simply unacceptable. So, armed with courage, conviction, and a firm resolve, she labored long and hard for what was known as "woman's suffrage." She died in 1906, almost a decade-and-a-half before her desired goal became achieved. But, perhaps without her relentless effort and unfailing perseverance, it would have been far later than 1920 before women citizens of the United States of America secured the right to vote.

It all began in 1872: In that time, a man was considered to be the complete master of the household. Women were able to earn money, but they could not necessarily keep it. According to law, if a woman was married and went to work, every penny she earned became the property of her husband.

In fact, a wife was viewed to be incapable of managing her own affairs. Since women were believed to be unable to think clearly, the law mercifully protected them by appointing guardians—male guardians, of course—over any property women might be lucky enough to possess.

In addition, women were not permitted to vote: This meant that women had no say in who would represent them in American democracy. Politicians tried to console women by saying that those officials elected by men would be magnanimous enough to take into consideration women's concerns as well, since men could share those with the officials in women's behalf. But it was clear that women had no power to be taken seriously—if you and I today do not think a politician is looking after our interests and reflecting our views sufficiently, we can vote that person out. Or if we feel a certain candidate today represents what we think is important, vital, and sensitive, we can vote that person in. We have the power that is so crucial to enable—in theory at least—representative government to be truly democratic. We can feel, more or less, that our views and interests are taken into account.

Women had no such feeling. Women had no such power. They were, to quote some magazines of the time, "the weaker sex," "the more delicate sex, "the emotional sex" (more than a few magazines said, "the irrational sex"); or to borrow the title of Simone de Beauvoir's best selling book, women were regarded as "The Second Sex."

Susan B. Anthony believed this to be unjust, inequitable, a violation of the Constitution of the United States, and even un-Christian. So, in 1872, she and 14 other women approached the voting polls and indicated that they wanted to vote in the election. Here's what Susan B. Anthony had to say—

> I've come here to vote for the President of the United States. He will be my President as well as yours. We are the women who bear the children who will defend this country. We are the women who make your homes, who bake your bread, who rear your sons and give you daughters. We women are citizens of this country just as much as you are, and we insist on voting for the man who is to be the leader of this government.

A few days after, Susan B. Anthony was arrested and brought before a judge, accused of having illegally entered a voting booth. "How do you plead?" asked the judge. "Guilty!" she cried. "Guilty of trying to uproot the slavery in which you men have placed us women. Guilty of trying to make you see that we mothers are as important to this country as are the men. Guilty of trying to lift the standard of womanhood, so that men may look with pride upon their wives' awareness of public affairs."

And then, before the judge could recover from this onslaught, she added, "The Constitution says that no person is to be deprived of equal rights under the law. Equal rights! How can it be said that we women have equal rights, when it is you and you alone who take upon yourselves the right to make the laws, the right to choose your representatives, the right to send only sons to higher education? You, you blind men, have become slaveholders of your own mothers and wives,"

Susan B. Anthony was guilty!

I wonder: If you and I were on trial, charged with being Christians, would there be sufficient evidence to convict us? If you and I were defendants facing the claim that we were followers of Jesus Christ, would there be enough testimony from witnesses to find us guilty?

The Letter of James clearly tells us that faith without works is dead. That is, our belief system demonstrates itself by outward actions of moral behavior and goodwill. So would we be guilty in a religious court by displaying ample evidence that we are guilty of loving God, of following Christ, and of loving our neighbor?

I find that science and religion come together here regarding this question in a powerful and helpful way: Ever since the time of Francis Bacon, science has proceeded in its investigation of the natural world by using the inductive method. That is, science proceeds from examining the particulars to reaching a general conclusion or theory. This induction, in turn, becomes a hypothesis which can be tested by continued observation.

To say that another way, science produces specific findings which can prove a general statement; there can be an inferring of the general from an examination of particular instances.

To use the scientific method in the arena of religious faith would mean that a person's life could be examined to see if there were enough particulars to reach a justifiable conclusion or inference that that person was indeed a Christian. Would there be a sufficient amount of things about *us* that scientists would observe and thereby lead them to the hypothesis that they have witnessed a Christian? Could the scientific method produce enough facts, enough particulars about you and me, to prove the general statement, "They are Christians"?

Of course, we are not perfect. But in the midst of our imperfections, in spite of our inevitable and all-too-human shortcomings, would there nevertheless be enough that would justify our being called "Christians"?

If we were put on trial for being Christians, would they have enough evidence to convict us? Would the foreman of the jury be able to say, "We find the defendant guilty as charged"? Would the judge be able confidently to declare, "There was no mistrial"? Would the spectators be able to remark, "The prosecution won hands down! Mr. Berger has finally triumphed against Mr. Mason! There's no denying it: The defendants are unquestionably guilty of being followers of Jesus Christ!"?

Scripture for reflection: Matthew 25:31; James 2:14-26

Hidalgo

In November of 1532, a steel-helmeted column of 62 cavalrymen, 150 foot soldiers, and a priest wound into the mountains of northern Peru. Lured by adventure and excited by gold, they were led by an aging explorer/former pig farmer who was both illiterate and illegitimate. His name is Francisco Pizarro.

In the words of one of the soldiers who wrote down his thoughts at the time, Pizarro and his men were *"tan soberbios como pobres, e tan sin hacienda como deseosos de alcanzarla"* ("as proud as they were poor, and as much without wealth as eager to achieve it").

Despite 10 years' planning and exploring, Pizarro's invasion of the Inca Empire of Peru was severely—one could easily say, ridiculously—undermanned: They had with them lances and Toledo-bladed swords, a few crossbows, some *arquebuses* (forerunners of the musket), and a couple of small cannon. His adversary, the Incan emperor, Atahualpa, commanded a huge army of 70,000-80,000 warriors.

How did those couple hundred Europeans acquire the nerve to invade an empire of six million inhabitants occupying a territory twice the size of their native Spain? What compelled them to embark—and succeed—in a venture that appeared illogical, if not suicidal? Was it simply and powerfully gold, "the sweat of the sun" as the Incas called it? Or was it more than that?

Indeed, the Spaniards' hunger for the yellow precious metal puzzled the Incas: To native South Americans, it was an aesthetic substance, valued because of its role in architecture and ritual. To the invaders, it was sought because of what it could buy. So obsessed with gold were the *conquistadores* that the Incas wondered whether the Europeans ate it!

Greed was but one of the Spaniards' compulsions. They were also driven by a fervent and strong religious faith, honed in holy war against the "Moors" (Muslims who had occupied southern Spain for 700 years). The invaders called themselves "Christians" more than they called themselves "Spaniards," and some referred to the Incan Indians as "Moors" and their temples to the sun god *Inti* as "mosques." If they were to lose their lives in this risky gamble, in this exciting extravaganza, would it not be in the service of the Cross?

"The daring of the Spaniards is so great that nothing in the world can daunt them," wrote the Spanish chronicler, Cieza. He continued in his journal, "No other race can be found which can penetrate through such rugged lands solely by the valor of their persons and the forcefulness of their breed without bringing with them wagons of provisions or tents in which to rest, or anything but a sword and a shield, and a small bag in which they carried food." Cieza was simply stating the hard facts, not making unwarranted boasts.

But the driving forces of avarice and faith do not fully explain the Spaniards' success. For beyond greed and daring lay a lust to be "somebody." Contributing to the invaders' ruthless single-mindedness and self-confidence was a desire to "become something," to make one's indelible mark in history and in society. Pizarro and many of his followers came from an area of Spain in which unemployed but adventurous riffraff roamed the countryside. Poor and uneducated, but proud and haughty, they bowed only to God and king. By their natural instinct and from the education-on-the-streets of the harsh frontier of west-central Spain, they were so aggressive that their natural response to danger was instant, murderous attack.

All of this was in the service of wanting to be "somebody." For these individuals could achieve fame and honor through their daring and resilience. In fact, several would win minor titles for brave deeds, titles granted by the king or by members of his court. Pizarro himself was named by Charles I, King of Spain and Holy Roman Emperor, as "Governor and Captain General of Peru." Each *conquistador* hungered for the title of *hidalgo*—"hijo de algo," "somebody."

In I Peter in the Bible, we learn that, in Christ, you and I have become somebody. Once we were nobody; but now, through Christ, we know that we are loved by God, we are shown mercy by God, and we are valued by God.

I suppose that each of us has had an experience at some point in our lives in which our value to others was questioned, unclear, ignored, or apparently non-existent: Maybe it was when people congregated in groups to do something, and we were left out. Or when people paired-off to go get something to eat, to be together, or to dance, and we were the "odd person out." We felt like we were nobody. We feared that we truly were nobodies. Our self-confidence was shaken, and our self-esteem was punctured. Flooded by self-pity, we felt that we were an "oversight" that had been overlooked.

But what the Bible is saying to you and me is, though the world at times treats us as worthless, as nobody, God regards us as somebody. When the world looks past us, God looks to us.

We know this because of Jesus. Jesus, whom the builders rejected as worthless, has been shown to be the chief cornerstone of the whole building. We, too, have been called from out of the darkness of distance from God into the light of God's close presence. Once we were *not* God's people, now we *are* God's people. Once we were nobody, now we are somebody!

Of course, the Spaniards were not the only persons who longed to be somebody. The Inca Empire itself was divided into two major classes—the nobility, the ruling class, was the somebodies; the masses were known as "worthless people." If the passage from I Peter had been originally directed to the people of Peru in the fifteenth century rather than to the people of the Middle East in the first century, it might have been phrased, "Once you were 'worthless people;' now you are Incas."

Once you were worthless; now you are Incas. Once you were nobody; now you are somebody. In his book, *Somebodiness: The Thought of Martin Luther King, Jr.*, Professor Garth Baker-Fletcher makes the point that historically the Christian faith gave Black folks a sense of worth and acceptance. Society may have treated Afro-Americans as if they were dirt; but Christ treated them as if they were saints. Through the week, Blacks had to suffer the indignities associated with their being different, their having black skin. But on Sundays in church, they were free from this persecution, and they were reminded that they were indeed, "valued 'somebodies.'" Once you were nobody; now you are somebody. Now you are "hidalgo."

Of course, the "somebody" that we are through Christ is not an identity based on power, wealth, or elitism. The Spanish were brutal and unforgiving in their devastation of Incan culture. That kind of unflinching savagery is *not* what it means to be "somebody in Christ." You and I are not free to treat others with viciousness or even merely with unkindness. Jesus, in whom we have our identity and from whom we gain our worth, says to "*love* your enemies" and to "pray for those who persecute you." Jesus does *not* say to obliterate those who stand against you and "beat the snot" out of those who pose even the slightest threat.

Our "somebodiness in Christ" is not based on power as the world knows it and power as the world wields it. Nor are we "somebody" because of the wealth we can amass. The Spaniards were inspired by gold and by silver, the "tears of the moon," as the Incas understood it. But Jesus confronts *us* with the question, "What does it profit a person, if you gain the whole world and forfeit your soul?"

Our culture says that who you are is symbolized by the car you drive, the clothes you wear, the friend you hang-out with, and the size of your bank account. You are 'somebody' in the eyes of the world if you can brag about all these considerations.

But Jesus says, "Not so!" Who you are is measured not by your cash but by your character, not by the extent of your wardrobe but by the size of your heart, not by the people who envy you but by the individuals on the edge that you care-about and serve, not by how you look but by how much you love, not by how greedy you are but by how grace-full you are willing to be.

Once you were nobody; now you are somebody. Now you are "hidalgo."

The "somebody" we are in Christ is not identified by our ruthlessness in autocratic power or by our affluence in terms of stockpiled possessions. Nor is the "hidalgo" we are in Christ measured by our elitism. Some people exhibit a smug arrogance in terms of their relationship with Christ: They are so proud (and so possessive) of their Christian commitment that they "lord their Lord" over everybody else. At times, it's almost as silly as one little kid teasing another by saying and claiming, "I've got Jesus, and you don't."

Rather than pumping-up our egos, we are humbled by Christ's acceptance of us. We know we did not deserve it; we did nothing to qualify for it, we did nothing to guarantee it. No, in spite of how we were (and what we did), Jesus found us worthy.

Therefore, we have a challenge. We have a challenge to say "thank you" to God and to Christ in a way that is fitting, in a manner that is appealing and pleasing and uplifting of ourselves and others. In the Bible, Ephesians 5 makes this point using the images of light and darkness: "You yourselves used to be in the darkness, but since then you have become people who belong to the light. For it is the light that brings a rich harvest of every kind of goodness, righteousness, and truth. Try to learn what pleases the Lord" (verses 8-10).

Our status as "hidalgos," as "somebodies-in-Christ-who-really-don't-deserve-it," compels us not toward elitist pride but to humble service. Our words tell others of Christ not in self-service ("we've got Jesus and you don't"), but in a genuine concern for the spiritual richness that a relationship with Christ brings. Our actions tell others of Christ not in self-aggrandizement ("look at how good I am"), but in a testimony to the power of loving kindness in a person's life. Our intentions tell others of Christ not to produce envy ("see what I'm going to have if all goes according to plan"), but to further the Kingdom goals of him who said, "I have come not to be served but to serve."

Once you were nobody; now you are somebody. You are "hidalgo."

Scripture for reflection: I Peter 2:4-10; Ephesians 5:8-20

Buried for Lack of Appreciation

Emperor Aurangzeb, the third of Shah Jahan's four surviving sons, was not a nice man! A puritan zealot for Islam, he wanted to establish the Islamic faith as *the* state religion of India. He had no time for music, painting, architecture, and history-writing. Denied imperial patronage, these pursuits withered.

Emperor Aurangzeb killed off his rival brothers one-by-one, and kept his father, who had built the beautiful Taj Mahal as a memorial to his beloved wife, in prison for seven years in the Agra Fort (from which his father would view the reflection of the Taj Mahal in a small piece of glass).

In a desperate plea to the Emperor's heart about the plight of the arts, some musicians from the capital initiated a funeral procession of music with loud wails that could not miss imperial ears. When asked what was going on, the mourners replied, "Your majesty," we are musicians, going out to bury our music for lack of appreciation." "Bury it *deep*," said the Emperor, "*so* deep that it never surfaces again."

And there began in India at that time, an eclipse of the arts, especially music.

Buried for lack of appreciation.

How many things do we bury for lack of appreciation? We sometimes bury *civility* toward one another because of the smug press of our individual identities and our personal points-of-view. I was recently on a college campus on the east coast where some minority persons had been sorely persecuted by the majority. So judgmental and distancing were persons in the majority that they were insensitive, unkind, and ignorant toward persons in the minority.

But the burial of civility did not stop there. The minority individuals, who had been so nastily treated, then acted toward the majority with the same kind of nastiness, unkindness, and incivility as they themselves had suffered.

"An eye for an eye, and the whole world goes blind," was the way Mohandas Gandhi put it.

Civility—buried for lack of appreciation.

In addition, we sometimes bury *excellence* for lack of appreciation. Face it, it's easy, it's tempting, it's dangerous, to settle for mediocrity. Just do enough to get by. Just do enough good stuff to pass. Just hold out enough compassion to avoid becoming totally calloused.

"If you are asked to go one mile, go two," said Jesus; "and if you are asked for your coat, give your cloak as well." But Jesus' words seem so often to go unheeded—are even un-heard—in a climate in which "the extra umph" to get beyond the superficial, the facile, and the mediocre is deemed silly, unnecessary, and inappropriate.

Excellence—buried for lack of appreciation.

We also sometimes bury *truth* for lack of appreciation. We know the truth, and the truth can set us free; but we occasionally prefer living in slavery. Our society enslaves us in a mad dash for who can accumulate the most and the best of worldly goods. The latest fashions, the latest technology, the brand-name athletic shoes, the hottest new download—we are told by our consumer society that, if we've got these, we are *somebody*.

In fact, you and I are bombarded thousands of times daily with the relentless message that our lives will gain cosmic happiness and meaning, if we simply drive the fastest car, splash on (or spray on) the sexiest aftershave (or perfume), drink the most popular beverage, show off the darkest tan, hang out with the hottest people, go to the most recently-released film, eat the juiciest steak, buy the best-selling brand, travel to the most-envied vacation spot, use the ultimate deodorant, brush with Consumer Report's top-rated toothbrush and toothpaste, and buy a cemetery plot with the prettiest view.

Never mind about character, how much cash do you have? Never mind about honesty, how are you going to get ahead? Never mind about method, did you win or not? Never mind about friends, whom did you use lately to your advantage?

Truth—buried for lack of appreciation.

> Civility—buried for lack of appreciation.
> Excellence—buried for lack of appreciation.
> Truth—buried for lack of appreciation.

Matthew 5 is that portion of scripture that contains the Sermon on the Mount. Some scholars have argued that these verses contain a summary of Jesus' message and therefore a summary of the Christian faith. One theologian called Matthew 5 "the epitome of all of the words Jesus ever spoke"—in other words, a composite of Jesus' teachings to his disciples over his entire ministry. If this is true, than we have in the fifth chapter of this Gospel according to Matthew, words that are intended to guide us, inspire us, correct us, and judge us: "Blessed are the poor in spirit, blessed are those who mourn, blessed are the meek, blessed are those who pursue righteousness, blessed are those who show mercy, blessed are the pure in heart, blessed are the peacemakers."

And later in Matthew 5, Jesus proclaims to his disciples,

> You are the light of the world. A city set on a hill cannot be hid. Nor is a lamp lit and put under a basket; rather it is placed on a stand, and it gives light to the whole house.

Several years ago, a group of college students and I visited an ancient Talmudic village in the north of Israel. Several houses that had been unearthed dated back to at least the second century A.D. Imagine the power of the experience of entering these houses made of stone that persons had inhabited more than 1800 years ago!

Inside one house, they had a clay lamp, placed on a stand—a kind of shelf—protruding slightly from the vertical surface of the walls. It looked like a saucer, with olive oil in it, and a wick floating on the top. This oil lamp functioned just as it had been used nearly two millennia ago. And, since it was not easy to kindle a light back then (for we have matches today), when persons left their homes in ancient times they placed the oil lamp—still burning—under a bushel basket. That allowed it to remain burning, but prevented an accidental fire that could destroy the houses.

Under the basket, the light was contained, hidden, "buried"—and could not be seen. But when the residents returned, the light was taken out, returned to the stand on the wall, and the entire house was lit-up. It amazed me while in the house in this Talmudic village that a small lamp could be so illuminating of the whole interior.

Jesus tells his followers that they (we) are the light of the world. Hidden—buried—under a basket, we provide no illumination. But placed on a stand, where our light can shine, we emit a radiance that spreads everywhere.

It strikes me that Jesus, who himself was the Light of the world (John 9:5), calls *us* the light of the world, too. And, when we are like Jesus, when his love shines from us to others, then we are deserving of this comparison.

But the question is, are we enough like Jesus to make the comparison justified? Do we let our light so shine that persons see the goodness and love within us and as a consequence are led to see God?

Maybe sometimes; but not enough! Too often we hide our light, either because we dim it because of our very un-Christian behaviors (our less-than-admirable actions and words), or we are embarrassed or uncomfortable letting others know *that* our faith is and *what* our faith is. Sometimes the light of our Christian faith is buried for lack of appreciation.

The function of a light is to be seen. The purpose of an oil lamp in an ancient house is to illumine. So how can our faith be better seen? How can we be more illuminating?

First, I would suggest that when we ourselves practice kindness and civility to one another (and to other persons who are not necessarily Christian) we allow our light to shine. Rabindranath Tagore, the Hindu poet, once remarked appreciatively of Christians, "They are persons who are kinder than necessary."

Would that *we* might be deserving of that commendation: "The Christian students, the Christian faculty, and the Christian staff persons at this College are kinder than necessary." When you and I strive hard to show forth sensitivity, compassion, and forgiveness, we illumine the campus, and civility and our Christian faith are not buried for lack of appreciation.

Second, I would suggest that when we strive for excellence in our lives and in all that we do, we send a powerful message to a campus and a world that are all too eager to settle for the easy way out, all too eager to make the irresponsible response, and all too eager to be content with mediocrity.

When you and I as Christians stand for excellence—excellence in and out of the classroom, excellence in everything we undertake—we allow our light to shine, exposing mediocrity for what it is, and allowing for the possibility that those who would settle for it might be inspired. And, as a result, excellence and our Christian faith are not buried for lack of appreciation.

Third, I would suggest that when we ourselves live-out the truth of our faith, we shine like a lighthouse. Our Christian light is to be a "guiding" light. So when we display the truth of our tradition, and in the process, provide an alternative to our consumer-driven, materialistic culture, we give guidance to others. The truth of our Christian faith—with its values of humility, service-to-others, and character-over-cash—can bring to light the inadequacy, the false promises, and the stale hopes of a society that itself values arrogance, self-promotion, and the size of one's bank account. When we live like the King (Jesus) rather than living like *a* king, we allow our light to shine, and truth and our Christian faith are not buried for lack of appreciation.

Civility, excellence, and truth are like the mourning musicians wailing to Emperor Aurangzeb. The culture asks, "What's going on?", and the virtues answer, "We are going to be buried for lack of appreciation." And culture replies, "Well, then bury yourselves *deep*, *so* deep that you will never be heard from again!"

But then Jesus says:

> You are the light of the world. A city built on a hill cannot be hid. No one after lighting a lamp puts it under a basket, but on the lamp stand, and it gives light to all in the house. In the same way, let your light so shine before others, that they may see your good works and give glory to God. (Matthew 5:14-16)

Scripture for reflection: Matthew 5:14-16

The Spring of Hope

> It was the best of times, it was the worst of times, it was the age of wisdom, it was the age of foolishness, it was the epoch of belief, it was the epoch of incredulity, it was the season of light, it was the season of darkness, it was the spring of hope . . .

These words are from the beginning of Charles Dickens' exciting and suspenseful novel, *A Tale of Two Cities*. It was the best of times, it was the worst of times . . . it was the spring of hope . . .

It was the best of times, it was the worst of times, for the disciples and other followers of Jesus in Jerusalem. The worst came first: It was dangerous for Jesus to go to Jerusalem, the political center of Israel and the religious vortex of Judaism. It was Passover, the roads to Jerusalem were jam-packed with traffic, and the city itself had swollen to several times its normal population. During this time of celebration and remembrance of the delivery of the Israelites from Egyptian bondage, there was an electric-like charge of energy in the capital city. The Jews focused this pilgrimage festival in the Temple, adjacent to the Antonia Fortress where the Roman soldiers kept watch on the religious activities. The soldiers were nervous: As a conquering and occupying force, they knew too well that the celebration of political freedom occurring within their field of vision was a powder keg waiting to explode. And Pontius Pilate, the local Roman ruler, who normally stayed in the lush, seaside, resort city of Caesarea Maritima had come up to Jerusalem to oversee crowd control and to maintain law and order, thus ensuring the *Pax Romana*, the Roman peace.

The priests—in cahoots with the Romans in order to keep their jobs running the Temple—were undoubtedly nervous, too. They knew that troublemakers from anywhere—and especially from that raucous area to the north, the Galilee—not only posed a threat to the Romans, but simultaneously to their job security. This was the deal they had cut with the Romans: They could keep their occupations, but it was their responsibility to report any rebellious act, any seditious person, to the authorities. The High Priest, Josephus Caiaphas, and the Roman ruler, Pilate, were thus collaborators for mutual benefit.

Pilate, in fact, was rather trigger-happy—not in terms of a gun, of course, but in regard to the Roman form of capital punishment, crucifixion. Crucifixion was not unique to the Romans in history, but they used it widely and as extremely as possible as a punishment for convicted criminals and as a deterrent to potential criminals and subversives. As a result, thousands of Jews were crucified in the first quarter of the first century. In this regard, the crucifixion-happy Pilate would be recalled to Rome after a decade of rule (26-36 A.D.) and put on trial, so excessive was his use of force and terror in his unrestrained desire to thwart disturbances and keep the peace. He was even, and obviously, too barbaric for the regularly-brutal Roman authorities themselves.

Jesus had caused a scene and quite a stir in the Temple during the days leading to Passover (according to the Gospels of Matthew, Mark, and Luke), and this brought him to the attention of the Temple authorities and subsequently placed him in the crosshairs of the Romans. The Romans would deal with him in the manner in which they dealt with all disturbers of the peace. And they did.

After one of Jesus' own band of followers—Judas—turned state's evidence, the Romans arrested Jesus, brought him before Pilate, and he was whipped and mocked. Made to carry his own cross, he was put to death outside the city walls of Jerusalem, so that passersby could see what happened to persons who went up against Roman power and authority.

Fellow Jews—Jewish officials—had accused Jesus of blasphemy, a charge punishable by death by stoning. But Pilate and the Romans could care less about blasphemy; after all they were polytheists (along with the pagan majority of the population of the Empire), not monotheists, and blasphemy was a religious matter. No, they cared about political matters, and were especially kneejerk-reactive to subversion, and revolutionaries, and persons who could disturb the peace. So, Jesus was crucified as a criminal and hung between two other criminals who had been sentenced as bandits and perhaps as murderers as well. The charge for which Jesus was crucified was being acclaimed as the Messiah, "the king of the Jews," a political title, for in this he was perceived to be a political threat. After all, he preached a lot about the Kingdom of God, in contradistinction to Caesar's kingdom; and God's kingdom was understood to be a this-worldly phenomenon in which God's will would be done on earth as it was in heaven, and God's reign would be established. Of course, the Romans did not believe for a moment that Jesus alone could topple the Roman imperial regime and install an alternative, divine rule! But *any* threat to the authority of this foreign, occupying power was dealt-with harshly. Better to put down something before it could get going, and better to do it quickly.

The remaining disciples went into hiding, fearing for their very lives. Perhaps what was done to their leader would be done to *them*. Their fearless second-in-command, Peter—upon whom Jesus said he would establish the Church—became so fearful for his own security and safety that he denied ever having had anything to do with the Jesus of Nazareth who was dispatched on that cruel instrument of capital punishment, the cross.

This had to be the low moment in the movement's history. The disciples thought they were coming to Jerusalem for a party and perhaps even a victory—what if the Kingdom of God would come at that very year's celebration of Passover, at that very moment in time? And now this: The execution of their leader, the disintegration of the movement, and the scattering of the major players. It was the worst of times.

You and I live in challenging and troubling times. Sometimes it appears to be the worst of times. Our society is incredibly violent: Each newscast details the use of violence, by robbers who break the law, and at times by police who are charged with upholding the law. Terrorists threaten our domestic security. Our society remains racist: Despite significant progress in race relations since the last century, race is still a powerful divider in American society—socially, economically, politically, and even sometimes religiously. It has been said that the most racist hour of the week is Sunday morning worship in churches.

And our world is incredibly violent: Each newscast details the use of violence by terrorists, dictators, and the rich and powerful who oppress the poor and weak. North Korea has developed nuclear plans, and Iran has been chastised and challenged by the world community for trying to do so also. It is dangerous to travel abroad, and it is dangerous to stay at home and travel domestically.

It is a dangerous and challenging world in which we live. The ecological disruption which our planet suffers, in the opinion of most scientists and environmentalists, is the worst in the history of the earth. We have too little of some natural resources, and we're producing too much pollution. The ozone layer "up there" in the stratosphere has a hole in it, and our trees "down here" in the rain forest are disappearing at the rate of a football field-sized area *per* minute. We have too many people being born, and not enough space for our garbage. The extinction rate of plant and animal species is going up, and acid rain is coming down

We live in a dangerous, challenging world.

Some would say, "The world is going quickly to hell in a hand-basket. See how far it has gone already!" The world is not lacking prophets of doom and gloom who see no hope at all. These doomsayers are as numerous as the plagues of Egypt!

On the other hand, we have some who, ignorant of the events that are the customary fare of life in the world and looking at the world in a skewed "Have a Nice Day" fashion, would say, "Everything's fine, thank you, none of this *seems* to be directly affecting me. All is well!" The world is not lacking naive Pollyannas who confuse uninformed elation with realistic hoping. These cheerleaders are as numerous as the tongues of Babel!

What seems to be *lacking* is a way of looking at the world, which sees not only the awful, sinful, violent side to life on the earth, but also sees and celebrates the realistic possibilities of hope.

It is the worst of times.

Of course, the worst of times did not stay that way for the disciples. We know how the situation turned-out: Good Friday was not the end of the story. Crucifixion was not the final word. For on the Sunday following Jesus' crucifixion, God undid what had been done. God reversed the pattern of evil winning, God overturned the tables (as Jesus had done in the Temple) of injustice and violence. God gave the victory to goodness over evil, to life over death, to triumph over tragedy. "In all things God is working for good," the Apostle Paul would proclaim (Romans 8:28).

So it was then the best of times. Hope had not been ultimately defeated, hope had not been finally deflated, hope had not been forever evaporated. First, it was the worst of times; then it was the best of times. Because of Easter, it had become the spring of hope.

And so the disciples came forth from their hiding places and began spreading the word that this Jesus who had been killed, was now alive, that this Jesus, who had met an untimely and unwarranted demise, had been raised from the dead by God. And Jesus' followers took the risk to proclaim that the risen Christ was, indeed, the Messiah and the Son of God. And they took their message to all who would hear and those who would not hear. Some paid the price with their lives. But their courage had been inflated, their allegiance rekindled, their loyalty reinvigorated. Having hidden in fear, they now fearlessly followed Jesus' command to "go and make disciples of all nations . . . " (Matthew 28:19).

Because of Easter, what are the springs of hope for us today? What are the seeds of hope in this dangerous, challenging world? What are the "springs of hope" that point to compassion, kindness, humility, and love, and can encourage us, give us direction, and transform the world even a little?

At the big homecoming football game at a school in Ohio, the young woman chosen Queen had just been "crowned." She turned, walked to another girl on the court, and put her crown on the girl's head. That girl's mom had just died that morning from a long battle against cancer. The now "former Queen" told the "new Queen" that she wanted to do this, both to honor the girl's mother and to lift the spirits of the daughter. The girls hugged each other, and both cried tears of happiness.

At a school in Kentucky, a young man confined to a wheelchair spear-headed a state-wide, with national links, effort to gather wheelchairs, crutches, canes, and walkers for kids like him in Third World countries who have no such aids for mobility. He was quoted as saying: "I have this neat wheelchair which gets me around. I can't stand the fact that other people have nothing."

In Phoenix, Arizona, a little boy named "Bobby" was diagnosed with fast-paced leukemia. The local fire department learned that his dream had been to become a fireman when he grew up. But now, of course, that dream had been dashed by the disease. However, the fire chief, a guy named "Bill," contacted Bobby's mother and asked if they could make him an honorary fireman with a real badge and a cool hat. She said, "Of course," and so they did. A couple months later, the mother phoned the fire department and told them that Bobby's end was drawing near. The firemen asked if they could come to the hospital and visit him. The answer, again, was "Of course." Fire chief Bill contacted the hospital, told them not to panic when they heard sirens and saw flashing lights, for there was no

A User-friendly Universe?

actual fire. Then the firemen rode their fire truck to the hospital, extended their ladder to the third floor where Bobby's room was, and, with permission from the hospital, entered that room through the window! Fourteen firemen and two firewomen came to Bobby's bed and hugged him and told him that they loved him. "Am I a real fireman?" Bobby asked. "You sure are!" fire chief Bill replied. And with that, Bobby smiled and closed his eyes for the last time.

It is the best of times when kindness, humility, compassion, and love are cultivated in response to the hope based on Easter and God's work in the world and our assurance that goodness will win out, that virtue will triumph, that love is eternal and is not lost even through death. It is the best of times when we vow that we'll make a positive difference in the world. And so—

> It is the best of times, it is the worst of times, it is the age of wisdom, it is the age of foolishness, it is the epoch of belief, it is the epoch of incredulity, it is the season of light, it is the season of darkness. It is the spring of hope.

Scripture for reflection: Matthew 27-28; Romans 8:31-39

Tariki-Jiriki

His birthday is April 8th. Born in a paradisal garden and into a golden net, his birthplace of Lumbini is in modern-day Nepal, a country north of India, and in the highest mountain range in the world, the Himalayas. His example and his teaching would change the course of Asian history, indeed, of world history.

His name is Siddhartha Gautama—Siddhartha meaning "wish fulfilling" and Gautama his family name, a royal family (for his father was a *raja*, a kind of "king").

The year of his birth was about 563 B.C., and he would live on earth for 80 years. Following an enlightening experience sitting under a wild fig tree when he was 35 years old, he became known thereafter as "the awakened one," "the enlightened one," or simply, "The Buddha."

April 8th is the Buddha's birthday, and on that day each year the 300-400 million Buddhists in the world remember and revere their founder.

In a number of ways, Siddhartha and Jesus are quite similar: Their followers established religions based on the centrality of these two persons, each taking the particular religion's name from the title of the individual "founder": Christians take their name from Jesus' title, the Messiah or *Christ*; Buddhists take their name from Siddhartha's title, The Awakened One or *Buddha*.

A User-friendly Universe?

Both persons were advocates of peaceful, non-violent means. Both were teachers (Jesus a rabbi, Siddhartha a guru), both were itinerant, both were leaders of a band of followers.

In a number of ways, however, they were quite different: Siddhartha came from a rich family, Jesus from a relatively-poor one. Siddhartha lived to old age, Jesus barely reached maturity. Siddhartha died from natural causes, Jesus was cruelly executed.

Throughout Buddhism and Christianity's respective histories, there has been an ongoing debate in each of them: The debate has emerged from trying to answer the question, How can one live in the kind of way that Jesus or Siddhartha models for his followers? What does it take for an individual to appropriate the salvation or solution-to-problems that these two historical figures offer? Does a person live a worthwhile life ultimately by drawing on his/her own powers or by appealing to a power or powers outside himself/herself?

To ask this question yet another way, "Is salvation for Christians and nirvana for Buddhists something that is 'given' or something that is 'gotten'? That is, is redemption (of whatever sort) the result of what you do for yourself or the result of what is done for you?

In my adopted country of Japan, Buddhism offers contrasting answers to these questions, which are involved in debate with each other: In Pure Land Buddhism, the believer relies on the grace of Amida Buddha so completely, that even saying his name ("Amida") on one's deathbed is sufficient to propel the follower into Paradise. So, the believer is dependent on another power rather than the power of the self to enter into Paradise.

But Zen Buddhism differs: Zen Buddhism emphasizes each individual's concentration (either through reflection on reason-defying sayings called "koans" or through sitting-meditation called "zazen") until enlightenment is achieved. So, the believer must depend on the power of the self rather than rely on an external power in order to achieve the goal.

The former (Pure Land Buddhism) stresses faith in the outside power, the power of the other. The latter (Zen Buddhism) stresses the works performed by inner power, the power of the self. The Japanese word for Other Power is "Tariki;" the Japanese word for Self Power is "Jiriki." "Tariki-Jiriki"—Other Power, Self Power.

So, according to Buddhism, is the desired goal accomplished as a gracious "gift" or as a "self-achievement"? Is enlightenment a 'given' or a 'gotten'? Is it something done for you or something you do for yourself? Buddhism would answer "yes." Yes, according to one tradition, it is something graciously presented perhaps even in spite of ourselves and our efforts; yes, according to another tradition, it is something that we work-for and accomplish in spite of outside distractions and interferences and barriers.

Before you begin thinking to yourselves, "Isn't Buddhism weird?" or "Those Buddhists talk out of both sides of their mouths!" or "So-what? Those Buddhists are confused, and I'm a Christian!," let's think together about Christianity:

How does one get saved in Christianity? How does a person come to redemption through Jesus Christ? How does one go to Heaven? How does an individual enter into the Kingdom of God?

In his Letter to the Galatians, Paul emphasizes that it is our faith that saves us. That is, God's grace accepts us in spite of our unacceptable actions and shortcomings. God does *for* us what we do not do (*cannot* do) for ourselves.

Paul implies that if we were left to our own devices, our own inner powers, we would fall short of being the kind of people God expects. And, indeed, when we see the pain and suffering that results from individual and corporate sin in the world, we concede that we too-often miss the target for which we were shooting (the word "sin"—*hamartia*—in Greek means to "miss the mark," as when an archer aims at a target and fails to hit it).

The Law (the teachings/commandments of *Torah*), therefore, says Paul, cannot save us: That is, since obeying all of the commandments in the Law is impossible for us as human beings (with our weaknesses and imperfections), the Law only illustrates our need for deliverance by a Power outside ourselves. Jiriki (Self

A User-friendly Universe?

Power) won't cut it, preaches Paul, because it *can't*; only the grace of God, Tariki—Other Power—can save us.

Paul puts it pretty bluntly: "Tell me just one thing," he writes to the Galatians; "did you receive God's Spirit by doing what the Law requires, or by hearing and believing the gospel? How can you be so foolish! You began by God's Spirit; do you now want to finish by your own power?" (Galatians 3:2-3)

In the previous chapter of Galatians, Paul had written, "We know that a person is put right with God only through faith in Jesus Christ, never by doing what the Law requires . . . do not reject the grace of God." (2:16a, 21)

Based on these scriptures, it appears that Tariki (Other Power) is what saves us. But then we must consider Matthew 25:

In this parable, Jesus announces judgment (whether one is saved or not) on the basis of "whether or not charity was withheld from the insignificant," as *The Anchor Bible Commentary* puts it. He points to his own identification with those who suffer and with the oppressed, and by implication highlights his ministry as an example par excellence of showing charity to the marginalized—the hungry, the thirsty, the stranger, the naked, the sick, and the imprisoned.

So, the "sheep" at his right hand—i.e., those who fed the hungry, gave the thirsty a drink, took-in the stranger, clothed the naked, ministered to the sick and visited the imprisoned—will go into eternal life and "inherit the Kingdom" (Matthew 25:46, 34). But the "goats" at his left hand—i.e., those who withheld charity from the insignificant—will go into eternal punishment (Matthew 25:46).

It would appear here that good works are what qualifies Kingdom membership. The scripture passage says absolutely nothing about the faith of the persons who have been categorized as "sheep" and "goats." It does not mention God's grace, but rather human action. Those persons who have unknowingly served Christ by serving the helpless and the hopeless will be the ones who are saved.

A person's good works are the basis of judgment, the parable suggests, and not one's faith. What you yourself choose to do has implications for your eternal destiny: Choose well and be rewarded; choose poorly and be punished. It's up to you. Jiriki (Self Power) is what saves us.

We find this same debate in Paul's Letter to the Romans and in the Letter of James: In Romans 3, Paul says—

> God's way of putting people right with God has been revealed, and it has nothing to do with Law . . . God puts people right through their faith in Jesus Christ. God does this to all who believe in Christ . . . By the free gift of God's grace, they are put right with him through Christ Jesus who sets them free . . . A person is put right with God only through faith, and not by doing what the Law commands. God's grace leads us to the eternal life through Jesus Christ our Lord. (Romans 3:21a, 22, 24, 2; 5:21b)

Faith in Jesus Christ puts us right with God (and is the only thing that can do so), and God's grace (Tariki—Other Power) leads us to eternal life.

But just as we assume that the debate has been decided and the issue settled, we read the following words in James 2:

> My brothers and sisters, what good is it for a person to say, "I have faith," if that person's actions do not prove it? Can that faith save him? Suppose there are brothers or sisters who need clothes and don't have enough to eat. What good is there in your saying to them, "God bless you! Keep warm and eat well!"— if you don't give them the necessities of life? This is how it is with faith: If it is alone and has no actions with it, then it is dead . . . How was our ancestor Abraham put right with God? It was through his

actions, when he offered his son Isaac on the altar.
So you see that a person is put right with God by
what he does, and not because of his faith alone. For
just as the body without the spirit is dead, so also
faith without action is dead. (2:14-17, 21, 24, 26)

Faith without good works is dead. For that faith alone cannot save us.

The debate continued in the early Church between the pro-faith Augustine, who outlined the "fallen nature" of human beings (and consequently our incapacity to do anything good on our own) and the pro-works Pelagius, who stressed freewill and choice. Augustine was Tariki (Other Power)-oriented; Pelagius was Jiriki (Self Power)-oriented.

This debate erupted in all its fury in the 16th century Protestant Reformation. Martin Luther proclaimed that we are saved by faith alone (*sola fide*) and that the Letter of James is "an epistle of straw."

Luther's argument was ignited and fueled by the Roman Catholic Church's practice of indulgences, in which the accumulated good works of the saints in a "treasury of merit" were supposedly "tapped" to aid in persons' salvation. Luther was clearly "Tariki-oriented," the Catholic Church at that time, "Jiriki-oriented."

The debate continues in traditional Presbyterianism vs. traditional Methodism, in which the former takes Calvin's notion of the "utter depravity of human beings" (and hence our need for a free-and-gracious salvation from the outside) and the latter takes Arminius' notion of "human perfectibility" (and hence our accountability for how well we live our lives in the direction of perfection based on power from the inside). Tariki-Jiriki.

So, from a Christian perspective, is salvation something done for you or something you do for yourself? Is entrance into the Kingdom a "given" or a "gotten"? Is eternal life a gracious "gift" or a "self–achievement"?

As with Buddhism, it appears that the Christian answer is "yes": Yes, according to some traditions, salvation involves faith and an undeserved gift; and yes, according to other traditions, salvation depends on good works and intentional discipleship.

So which is correct? Who is right?

In an important way, *both* are correct. Salvation depends on God's grace *and* on our human action. God graciously accepts us, but we are expected to respond to God's grace with appropriate action. Tariki and Jiriki are dynamically related to one another. There is, there must be, a vital synergism between the two.

The Apostle Paul once advised, "Work out your own salvation with fear and trembling" (Philippians 2:12). On his deathbed over 500 years before Paul was born, the Buddha's last words were, "Strive earnestly to work out your own salvation." My advice for you is the same!

Scripture for reflection: Galatians 3:1-14; Matthew 25:31-46

Keeping Sabbath throughout Our Lives

In the classic and now "ancient" movie, *Chariots of Fire*—which won an Academy Award for Best Picture of 1981 and is based on a true story—Eric Liddell is a Scottish runner for Great Britain in the 1924 Olympic Games in Paris. A very fast athlete, he grew-up in a family which would not do anything but go to church on Sundays—no non-religious activities such as playing games, attending concerts, playing with friends, and certainly no athletic competition, were permitted.

So when he is scheduled to compete in the 100-metre Olympic race on a Sunday, he decides out of conscience to withdraw. This allows a Jewish teammate, whose Sabbath was Saturday and not Sunday, to run in his place. This teammate, Harold Abrahams, wins the gold medal in the 100 metres, and then Liddell quite unexpectedly wins gold in the 400 metres on a subsequent day.

Sunday was a "day of rest," Eric had been taught. Sunday was the "Christian Sabbath," which should be "remembered" and kept "holy."

When I learned about this story as a young boy, I found it objectionable. In fact, I thought that *all* the days of the week were created by God and were therefore holy. And yet, I reflected, we do not regard every day as a "day of rest," because if we did, no work would ever get done at all!

And beyond this, I wanted to have fun, and the other six days of the week just didn't seem adequate to hold all the enjoyment that a young kid desired. So why couldn't I do fun stuff also on Sunday?

Despite my youthful objection, there is something appealing about one day *per* week which is relieved of the busyness, the hustle-bustle, the helter-skelter, of our typical schedules: One of the biggest complaints I hear from my friends, one of the most frequent gripes that I hear regularly on college campuses, is that people just don't have enough time. There's so much to do—so many books to read, papers to write, meetings to attend, rehearsals and practices to which to go, friends with whom to spend time, romances on which to work, jobs to be performed, and workouts to get into our schedules.

All these activities produce stress and leave us stressed-out. So why aren't we more eager, why aren't we more *intentional*, about building-in some "down time," some time to rest, some moments to rejuvenate?

Perhaps one reason is the pervasive impact of the Protestant work ethic: We work hard because we believe that that's what God wants, and even more, that that's what God *rewards*. Perhaps if we work really hard, God will give us good things, and we'll be acceptable to God. Perhaps if we work relentlessly, we'll deserve God's relentless love. Perhaps if we work ourselves to exhaustion, we'll merit God's inexhaustible grace.

Of course, we forget here that God doesn't love us because we work hard. God loves us because God loves us. As a result, we don't *earn* God's love. We try to lead good, moral lives, and we work hard at what we do as our way of saying "thank you" to God for God's loving us in the first place.

But still, we have ingrained in us that hard work pays off (it can, and usually does!), and that hard work will get us what we deserve (it can, but it doesn't make us deserving of God's love and grace!).

So, perhaps one reason we aren't so intentional about orchestrating some "Sabbath" time is because we believe we ought to be working all the time and thereby earning God's love.

Perhaps another reason is the "negative image" that the Christian Sabbath—Sunday—has suffered. Anything that is fun is not holy. Any activity save worship and Bible study is inappropriate. According to this image, Christianity is a faith based on not doing things that you shouldn't do. Following the Sabbath is a killjoy.

Of course, there *is* discipline in the Christian life. Being a Christian means saying "no" to nastiness and "yes" to kindness, it means declining hate and affirming love, it means turning away from selfishness and embracing sharing.

But being a Christian also means reveling in love, basking in grace, soaring in hope, and floating on divine presence!

Still, we have to overcome the negative caricature that has arisen—somewhat deservedly—regarding the Christian Sabbath.

Perhaps another reason is that our culture has encroached on Sabbath time. Malls are open on Sundays, soliciting our purchases and our accumulation of more stuff. Sporting events are bombarding the airwaves of our televisions. Churches often have meetings of church leaders and youth groups and conduct shut-in visitations and hospital checks on Sundays. Does this mean that there is not *any* time for us to rest?

Of course, church meetings and activities have to be held. And sometimes, Sundays happen to be the best (or the only possible time) for them.

But being a Christian means managing our time, and if we spend all our time "doing," then we cannot devote any of our time "reviving" our bodies and "rejuvenating" our souls.

It is clear that the notion of "time off"—of rest—of Sabbath—is emphasized throughout the Hebrew Bible. Every Sabbath is to be an occasion for physical and spiritual recuperation . . . not just for humans, but for every living thing in creation, including the land. After all, God rested on the seventh day after the initial six days of creation (Genesis 2:2-3). And every seventh year—the sabbatical year—the fields are to lie fallow. And every Jubilee year—the fiftieth year after seven cycles of seven years—slaves are to be set free, debts are to be written-off, and the land is to be redistributed. In other words, everybody and everything get a fresh start. "Behold the new has come and the old has passed away" (Revelation 21:5a).

So what are we to make of "keeping Sabbath throughout our lives"?

For whatever reason, Sunday itself may not be able to be our "sabbath time." But we must understand its function within the seven-day week—spiritually and physically—and we must intentionally carve-out some time and space to allow our souls to be refreshed and our bodies to be rested.

We cannot continue to beat ourselves "up" and "down" by never-ending labor and always-oppressive stress. The price we pay is too great—we shorten our lives, we lower the quality of our work, we erode our creativity, and we increase our impatience and our brittleness and our pessimism.

One wise person told me a formula for *each* day that I have found helpful. The wisdom goes like this:

> Every day, do one thing you must do, but which you don't really want to do. Every day, do one thing that you enjoy doing. Every day, do one thing just for *you*.

The "thing for you" could be taking a walk, lying down for a nap, reading something in no way related to your coursework or to your job, calling someone whom you like or love, hearing someone say to you that they like you or love you, writing a journal entry about your life, listening to music, playing music, singing, taking a run, painting a picture, snapping a photograph, hitting a golf ball, sending someone a note, walking the dog, sitting in the sun, taking a drive, buying some ice cream, playing some cards, going dancing, seeing a movie.

As theologian Dorothy Bass reminds us in *Practicing Our Faith*, "We need Sabbath, even though we doubt that we have time for it." Perhaps if we observed a little bit of Sabbath *each* day, we could momentarily and enjoyably step off the treadmill of work to find reinvigoration and peace.

And then we would be able to follow God's commandment to "remember the Sabbath." We would be able to "keep Sabbath throughout our lives."

Scripture for reflection: Exodus 20:8-11

The Erratic Behavior of Lunatics

It is tempting to provide the "standard interpretation" of the "story of talents" from Matthew 25—i.e., what God has given to you, *do something with*. The story is familiar to us: The master of the household is going on a trip, so he summons his three servants. To each of them, he gives some money—five talents, two talents, one talent—according to their abilities and potential. (I should probably add that "a talent" was no small sum of money; it was worth more than 15 years' wages of a laborer!). After being gone for some time, the master returns and asks how the servants have done with the money he had entrusted to them. The one with five talents made five talents more, for a total of ten talents. The one with two talents made two talents more, for a total of four talents. But the one with just one talent had dug a hole and hid the talent there. Now the master was overjoyed with the good care that had been provided by the first two servants, and he placed them in high positions of responsibility overseeing many things. But the master was outraged with the poor care that had been provided by the third servant. He gave him a "talking-to" and declared that he was a "wicked and lazy servant!", and then threw him out of the house!

And so, the message is pretty clear—do something with the gifts God has given to you, or else! And the interpretation is pretty easy and quite familiar. But perhaps it is too easy. For it is quite reductionistic:

A User-friendly Universe?

Since God's Word is eternal, it must speak afresh to life in the 21st century, as well as the 1st. For God's Word to be relevant, it must speak to issues and struggles we face in our daily lives—as individuals, as a community, as a nation, as a world.

These issues and struggles are multiple—the economy, racism, war, health care, terrorism, education . . . and the environment.

But one of these issues we don't feel as palpably as the others. It doesn't necessarily impact us as directly and fully as losses in our 401K plans, the killing of Black men on our streets, soldiers returning with post-traumatic stress disorder from multiple tours of duty overseas, the 47 million U.S. citizens with no health care, fear surrounding the threat of terrorism, and the rising costs of a college education with federal and state monies not keeping pace. And unless we pay attention to air quality alerts, or debate whether to drink bottled water or water directly from the tap, or keep track of logging in our national forests, or feel compelled to check the status of the dumping of waste by companies into the Great Lakes or note how fast our garbage dumps are filling-up—the concern about the environment is likely to elude us.

Be that as it may, what we are doing to the planet, to the Earth, to nature, to the Creation, to God's handwork, to our earthly home, can be encapsulated in the following way, in this pairing of opposites—

> acid rain is coming down, while garbage dumps are filling up; species are going extinct, while the human population is burgeoning; the ozone layer is thinning, while air pollution is thickening; global temperatures are increasing, while the rainforest is decreasing; oil is running out, while oil spills are running loose; prohibition against blowing-off the tops of mountains is headed nowhere, while toxic waste is headed anywhere that will take it.

What did Chief Seattle reputedly say in the 1854 letter attributed to him? "Foul your own bed, and you will suffocate in your own waste."

Unfortunately, most persons don't think that these environmental problems are very important. After all, who of us takes note of all of these? How many of us witness acid rain killing trees and fish? How many of us follow the garbage truck to the dump to see how much waste we produce and then have to get rid-of? How many of us live among a dense population whose poverty-existence is caused by so many people struggling with such limited resources? How many of us count the number of species we lose to extinction caused by human presence on the planet? How many of us worry about harmful ultraviolet rays from the sun or melting ice caps and glaciers? How many of us pause to think twice about air and water quality, for we just keep on breathing it and drinking it? How many of us have aerial photos which chart the loss of trees in the rainforest or in the national forests of the United States?

But then God's Word comes to us, just when we thought we had rationalized it away, just when we acknowledged that our typical everyday experience does not bump up against these problems, just when we thought that we could think about something else, just when we believed that what we don't know won't hurt us and what we don't see just doesn't exist.

God's Word asks us this question: "What have you done with the 'talents' with which I left you (*not* talents as personal abilities and aptitudes, not even talents as money which God has asked us to invest, but instead 'talents' as the resources of God's good earth that God has entrusted to us)?"

God asks, "What have you done with my creation which I have placed in your care? What have you done with what is mine, yet what I have given-over to you for the time being? What kind of a steward have you been?"

Now I know that stewardship—just like this biblical text of the "talents" from Matthew 25—often gets reduced to the Annual Fall

Fund Drive of any church. I know that the fall is normally the time when we assess how much money we will contribute to next year's church budget, when we decide how much time, and how much talent, as well, we are able to donate to the church.

And this is important! The stewardship committees of all the churches believe that it is *very* important. So what I am saying is *not* that it is unimportant; what I am saying is that that notion of stewardship is reductionistic—it is not enough; it is not even fully biblical.

To be a "steward" in the biblical sense means to be responsible for the care of God's creation. When the New Testament Greek word, *oikonomous*, needed to be translated in the seventeenth century in England, the word that was used is "stigwarde." Our modern word—"steward"—comes from the Old English word, stigwarde. "Stigwarde" referred to the person responsible for the welfare of the communal herd of pigs in a town. Each farm brought its pigs together into one large herd so that they could be looked-after and safely-defended. The stigwarde was the person who was entrusted with looking-out for the safety and care of those pigs. This was critical, for the economy of the town depended on the status and security of its communal pig herd. The stigwarde, the steward, was responsible to the whole town for what happened to the pigs.

This is biblical stewardship—not just what we do with our money, our time and our talents, but what we do with/to God's creation! So that when God returns and asks for an accounting, we can reply, "We have been *good* caretakers of what you entrusted to us. We have been faithful stewards. We have been dutiful 'stigwardes.' We have served the creation which you made and placed (literally) in our hands! Just as Christ served *us*, we have served other species and used natural resources wisely and defended the earth against degradation and exercised caution against exploitation. Just as you, God, loved the world so much that you were moved to give your only Son for it, so we have loved the world to such an extent that we were moved to care for it and defend it against abuse and misuse."

To do this, we must read Genesis 2 and heed it. We have internalized all too well Genesis 1; but we must also note Genesis 2. Whereas Genesis 1 says that we are to "have dominion and subdue the earth," Genesis 2 says we are to "till and tend" the Garden. The Hebrew word for "till" is *abad*. *Abad* means "to serve" or "to care-for." In fact, when the Bible talks about Israel as the servant of the Lord, or when we Christians believe that Jesus is the fulfillment of Old Testament prophecy as the servant of God, the Hebrew Bible words that are used are *ebed Yahweh*. *Ebed* is the noun "servant;" *abad* is the verb "serve." So, humans were placed by God in the Garden to "till it"—to *abad* it, to *serve* it. And the Hebrew word for "tend" is *shamar*. *Shamar* means to protect, and to defend. Every time a city is protected and defended by Israelite soldiers and townspeople in the Old Testament, the word used is *shamar*. So, "to till and to tend" really means—originally meant—"to serve and to protect."

These directives in Genesis 2 must not be forgotten, and must be creatively placed in-tension with the more aggressive, more militant language of Genesis 1, "have dominion and subdue."

For after all, we must recognize and we must confess that the earth is not ours; it is God's. "The earth is the *Lord's* and the fullness thereof," as Psalm 24:1 puts it. As a result, if it is God's, then it is not ours, and we can't do to it, we can't do with it, whatever we please. We can't use it for whatever we want. It doesn't belong to us; it's not our possession. We simply have it as a gift, a trust, a holding—for which we are responsible when God checks-in and checks-up on us.

Mary Westfall, a college chaplain, tells the following story in a book she co-edited, entitled, *The Greening of Faith*:

> I am reminded of a warm spring day in New York City, where I served my first pastorate fresh out of seminary. The pace of the city and the demands of my work often tested my theology and stretched my capacity to feel connected to God's good earth, its seasons, cycles, and miraculous ability to heal

the weary spirit. On that particular day, feeling in need of rejuvenation, I wandered into Riverside Park to sit and gaze at the Hudson River and try to regain my perspective. Moving off the noisy street, I found a quiet bench. Only a few moments later, while my mind was still preoccupied by the tasks that awaited my return, I noticed a disheveled-looking man moving along the sidewalk not far from me. His dirty clothing, incoherent ramblings, and characteristic plastic bag quickly identified him as one of the city's many homeless who spent their days gathering discarded cans and bottles to redeem at day's end. After diverting my eyes for a time, my gaze eventually wandered back to this "lost soul" just as he stooped to examine an object on the ground not twenty feet from me. I then noticed that it was not merely another aluminum can his hand now cradled, but a young bird, apparently having fallen from its nest in the branches above. To my utter amazement, the man muttered a few words, apparently to the tiny creature, then tenderly lifted it back into the tree, returned to his "work" and disappeared off into the park. Later that afternoon, I shared the experience with a colleague, who responded that this was clearly the erratic behavior of a "lunatic," discounting my suggestion that what I had witnessed was a human being living in the midst of the holy and aware of it. To this day, that nameless stranger remains for me a symbol of something many of us have lost [pp. 219-220].

"The erratic behavior of a lunatic." Or, the behavior of a "steward" of God's creation—one who was touched by the plight of a fellow creature and who did something positive about it. He suspended his search for redeemable aluminum cans—more "stuff" to make him a little bit of cash at day's end—and redeemed the precarious life of a defenseless bird. By caring for, and protecting, the baby bird by moving it up and away from harm, he showed himself to be a person who served God's creation.

So, you and I need to engage in the erratic behavior of lunatics! I think we *should*. But how can we?

Here are a few suggestions? Here are a few ideas for how you can become "lunatics":

> vigorously participate in any recycling program that is available— if it can be recycled, don't throw it away;
>
> turn out the lights when you are not in the room;
>
> turn off the tv when you are not watching it;
>
> read up on an environmental problem that concerns you—it may be affecting you, or someone that you love;
>
> watch the Nature channel, the Animal channel, the History channel so you can learn something about how nature works, how marvelously splendorous and beautiful God's creation is, and how we humans impact that splendor and beauty in negative ways;
>
> take a walk, and pay attention to what you see as you walk—look up at the sky, look at the trees, look for animals, check-out the insects;
>
> join the Audubon Society or the World Wildlife Fund or another environmental organization;

A User-friendly Universe?

take reusable bags with you to the grocery store and refuse to use the plastic ones that they would otherwise give you—bags that take hundreds if not thousands of years to decompose in garbage dumps;

write a letter to the Congressman of your choice, encouraging him/her to work toward alternative energies—it's not only wise environmentally, it's also wise economically and politically;

feed the birds during the winter months, when snow makes it difficult for them to find food;

subscribe to *National Geographic Magazine*, *Orion Magazine*, or *E* (Environmental) *Magazine*. Buy *Time* magazine's book, *Planet Earth: An Illustrated History*, at the bookstore of your choice;

purchase some plants for your room or your house, and "befriend" them as you take care of them—if it weren't for plants, there would be no oxygen for you to breathe, so "be kind" to them: Your life depends on it!;

purchase biodegradable substances for use around where you live;

visit a zoo, and notice how diverse the natural world is—while there, pay attention to which species, and how many species, are "endangered";

report anyone who dumps toxic substances down storm drains—it's not just illegal, it's also harmful to nature because those storm drains channel their contents into streams and rivers;

turn off the water when you are brushing your teeth and take shorter showers and briefer baths;

do an energy audit of where you live—how can you "lighten your footprint" on nature's resources and your pollution and waste?.

These are just a few recommendations for you to consider. Use your imagination: You can think up other ideas. You can come up with things that are relevant and meaningful to you as "lunatics."

Do it for nature. Do it for yourself. Do it for one another. Do it for God. For God's ready to ask, "What have you done with the 'talents'?" "What have you done with the creation that I entrusted to you?"

Scripture for reflection: Matthew 25:14-30; Psalm 24; Genesis 1-2

3-D Glasses

I love watching movies in an IMAX theatre. A few years ago, I went to see a "nature extravaganza" movie that transported the viewer over Victoria Falls in southern Africa. The experience was made even more realistic by the fact that the movie theatre dispensed 3-D glasses to every person entering.

The lenses of 3-D glasses make the images on the screen appear to leap right out at you! Viewers duck to avoid avalanches that seem to thunder right off the screen and onto them. Moviegoers shriek as they follow skiers down precipitous slopes at breakneck, breathtaking speeds.

The secret of 3-D effects lies in the way the lenses of the glasses unify two different images projected onto the screen simultaneously. When moviegoers don the special glasses, they are able to see everything from both perspectives at the same time, bringing the objects on the film to life. And that is what's so thrilling, so real, so powerful.

If one pays careful attention to the New Testament stories about Jesus and his disciples, she realizes that seeing from two perspectives is, in a sense, what Jesus asks of his followers. Jesus asks those who call themselves "Christians" to see things with two images projected simultaneously onto the world. Naturally, we Christians would continue to see the world we have always lived-in—the world of our senses, the world of politics and poverty and violence, the world of hard knocks, and 'real' life, and solid, indisputable facts.

This world is a world we have come to know all too well—a world of cancer snuffing out people's lives, and hungry people with nothing to eat, and homeless people with nowhere to go, a world of racism and sexism, a world of hate crimes, terrorism, and exploitation.

I don't think Jesus failed to see this side of the world in which he lived, in which *we* live as well: He knew all too well about the poor and the have-nots (90% of Judea and the Galilee, the two regions of Israel/Palestine in Jesus' time, were poor peasants while wealth was concentrated in the hands of only 10%); he knew about the marginalized Samaritans (he told a parable about one, a Samaritan who was *good*, which would have been unthinkable to first-century Jews); he knew about untouchable lepers; he acknowledged the hated tax collectors (he even had one in his band of disciples); he was aware of the ostracized women who were forced into, or who chose, prostitution (only two vocations were available to women in his time—being a wife or being a prostitute). He knew that the Roman political stability—the *Pax Romana* (the "Roman Peace")—was able to be maintained only by barbarous acts of brutality: Jesus would know about the Roman government and its habit in Palestine of crucifying troublemakers and rabble-rousers.

But Jesus also saw and knew another world as well. And he asked, *expected*, that his followers would learn to see also this world of God's envisioning—a world of happiness, justice, peace, and sharing, a world where there was war no more, selfishness no longer, sorrow not anymore, and stinginess had been given-up.

This world—this "preferred reality" (to use a Latin American theologian's phrase)—Jesus called "the kingdom," *God's* kingdom. And so the Bible reader, and the Bible scholar, quickly notice in spending time with the Gospels, that Jesus talks a lot about the Kingdom of God.

Now, it would not be correct to contend that Jesus was the *first* to talk about God's kingdom. As Professor John Killinger notes, the Kingdom of God had been envisioned as early as the time of

A User-friendly Universe?

Moses, when the Torah ("The Law;" "The Teachings") was given to the runaway slaves in the wilderness on Mt. Sinai. Torah—the first five books of what we Christians call the "Old Testament" (Genesis, Exodus, Leviticus, Numbers, and Deuteronomy)—talked about a time when there would be a divine kingdom on earth in which the strong would care for the weak (rather than take advantage of them) and when the rich would share with the poor (rather than exploit them). Torah talked about an order of things in which hospitality would be automatically and indiscriminately extended, and talked about a reality in which people who were different—in terms of nationality, physical challenges, marital status, and economic strata—would be respected rather than dissed.

Clearly, of course, God's kingdom does not absolutely nor completely govern the world today, any more than it did in Jesus' day. But that did not inhibit Jesus from talking about God's kingdom nor from believing it would one day completely arrive. In a section of the Gospel of Mark (second in order among the Gospels in the New Testament, but the first to be recorded, in about 70 A.D.), we find Jesus talking about the Kingdom of God. He uses this parable to convey his meaning:

> With what can we compare the kingdom of God . . . ?
> It is like a mustard seed, which, when sown upon the ground, is the smallest of all the seeds on earth; yet when it is sown, it grows up and becomes the greatest of all shrubs, and puts forth large branches, so that the birds of the air can make nests in its shade. (Mark 4:30-32)

Be that as it may, it is understandably hard to believe that the Kingdom of God can co-exist with a world of evil, pain, and suffering. Is the Kingdom present in a small way in the ethnic strife in so many places in the world today? Is the Kingdom of

God already-present in the stomachs of the 1,800 children of the world who will die each hour today from a lack of nutrition? Is the Kingdom of God present where there are drug dealers in high school, weapons on the playground, and drive-by shootings? Was the Kingdom of God present several years ago when a Black man was dragged to his death behind a pick-up truck by members of a white supremacist hate group in Alabama? Was the Kingdom of God present when six million Jews were exterminated in Hitler's gas chambers in eastern Europe? Was the Kingdom of God present when Jesus was killed on a cross outside the city walls of Jerusalem?

It is not easy to believe that the Kingdom of God can co-exist with our world. But Jesus was insistent on the Kingdom's presence and its mysterious power. And Jesus said that he expects his followers to live *as if* they see this Kingdom, this Kingdom of God, at the same time they are seeing the world as it is. That's like wearing 3-D glasses to allow one to see two different images or perspectives projected onto the same screen of reality at the same time. Jesus said that those who have faith are to live *as if* they see this Kingdom of God, for it is through our faith in this vision, this dream, this preferred reality, this divine Kingdom, that God works in the world. In fact, we pray regularly, the prayer Jesus taught us: "Our Father who art in heaven, hallowed be thy name. *Thy kingdom come, thy will be done, on earth as it is in heaven . . .*"

And who is to say that the Kingdom of God *hasn't* come, that it *isn't* here, when we behave *as if it were?*

This may have been part of what Jesus was trying to teach us: When we wear our religious 3-D glasses and see the world through the eyes of the Kingdom, the Kingdom is actually here in our midst in a small way, like a mustard seed—and if we act *"as if"* the world belongs more truly to God every time we act, then God's Kingdom is more completely present in the world—it grows and will eventually become a large tree.

A User-friendly Universe?

I think of persons who see the world through 3-D glasses:

> Mother Teresa, the Albanian nun, whose short stature was contrasted by a huge heart of compassion and service;
>
> Mohandas Gandhi, whose vision of non-violence led India to independence and inspired other persons to accomplish change through loving resistance;
>
> Rosa Parks, whose tired feet kept her from succumbing to unjust laws regarding seating on Montgomery city buses;
>
> Cesar Chavez, who organized migrant workers to protest their exploitation by the rich and powerful;
>
> Martin Luther King, Jr., who told us that persons' worth lay in the strength of their character rather than the size of their bank account or the color of their skin;
>
> Rigoberta Menchu, the Guatemalan *campesina* (or peasant) who stands for dignity and justice;
>
> Thich Nhat Hanh, the Buddhist peacemaker who works for respect and reconciliation around the world;
>
> Mbarak Awad, known as the "Palestinian Gandhi," who has sought a just and non-violent solution to the conflict in Israel.

These persons act *as if* the Kingdom of God is real in our world, and through their efforts it comes to be more fully present.

So, how can *we* see the world with 3-D glasses and act *as if* the Kingdom of God is real and in our midst?

> People will tell us that kindness is syrupy and wimpy—be kind anyway!;
>
> People will tell us that hope is wishful thinking by the melon-headed—be hopeful anyway!;
>
> People will tell us that serving others is passé and takes attention from what *really* matters . . . ourselves!—be a servant anyway!;
>
> People will tell us that denying ourselves unlimited acquisition of "stuff" is for the simple–minded—live simply anyway!;
>
> People will tell us that humility is for the weak and the losers—be humble anyway!

When we wear 3-D glasses and look at the world, we see the presence of the Kingdom of God in the world. When we wear 3-D glasses and look at the world, we participate in the work of God in the world. When we wear 3-D glasses and look at the world, we see the world as it could be. When we wear 3-D glasses and look at the world, we make a difference in people's lives in the world. When we wear 3-D glasses and look at the world, we make the world a little better than it was when we found it.

3-D glasses—*wearing 'em* makes all the difference in the world.

3-D glasses—wearing 'em makes *all the difference in the world!*

Scripture for reflection: Mark 4:26-34

Somewhere Under the Rainbow

In the ever-popular musical, "Wizard of Oz," Judy Garland as "Dorothy" sings these lines:

> Somewhere over the rainbow, way up high,
> There's a land that I heard of, once in a lullaby.
> Somewhere over the rainbow, skies are blue,
> And the dreams that you dare to dream,
> Really do come true.

Of course, Dorothy's search for a dreamland over the rainbow took her to the Land of Oz and the Emerald City with all of its superficial glitz and glitter ("This isn't Kansas, Toto!"). However, life in the Emerald City proved to be hollow and harrowing, and Dorothy longed to return home to her small town in Kansas. She preferred the past. So her land beyond the rainbow lay not in the *future*, but in the idealized *past* of her childhood.

> Somewhere, over the rainbow, way up high.

There are, of course, rainbows in the Bible as well. The rainbow in Genesis 9 was placed in the sky by God as an affirmation of the continuing covenant between God and all of the creation: Out of death and destruction had come new life; out of chaos and confusion had come created order. The biblical rainbow seemed to advise, "You've got to hang in there, something better's coming."

The difference between the rainbow in "The Wizard of Oz," and the rainbow in the Book of Genesis is striking: In the movie, the rainbow is a sign of human longing. In the Bible, the rainbow is a sign of God's promise. In the movie, the rainbow is associated with going back home to the familiarity (though over-valued), the security (though over-estimated), and the innocence (though idealized) of the *past*. In the Bible, the rainbow is the symbol of God's promise to be faithful to the creation as it moves toward the *future*.

The Wizard of Oz is a *delightful* movie—one of my all-time favorites—so I am not trying to find fault with it. But the biblical rainbow gives-in neither to the romantic nostalgia for the past that pervades the movie, nor to a bitter cynicism that tempts us when our hopes for something that we wanted badly have been dashed.

Professor Dan Migliore related an experience he had in the inner city of Trenton, New Jersey. While working with 9- and 10-year-olds, Dr. Migliore was asked to read a story from the Bible. He read to them the story of Noah and the rainbow. When he finished, he asked the children, "Where do you look to see a rainbow?"

The children replied, "We see rainbows on the street." Thinking that they had misunderstood him, Professor Migliore repeated the question, "Where do you look to see a rainbow?" "On the streets," the children said again; "you can see rainbows in the oil slicks on puddles in the streets and parking lots."

These children found hope in the midst of the mundane, the every-day, and the common sights of daily life in their neighborhood. They found rainbows in places no one would expect to look.

At times, we understandably ask *ourselves*, "Where is our *hope*?" "What hope can we reasonably have?" "Where is the source of hope in our lives?"

Christian hope (one of the "seven cardinal Christian virtues") is neither "chirpy optimism" nor "cynical pessimism": "Chirpy optimism"—the naïve Pollyanna—refuses to face the reality of human existence in the world. Despite our preference for it, life is *not* one vast Disneyland—we do not move in life from one intense experience of euphoria and excitement to another. No, life has its tragic dimension, whether disappointment, or disease, or accidents, or unexpected failure.

On the other hand, "cynical pessimism"—the despairing defeatist—is so immersed in the heaviness of life and so overwhelmed by negatives that there does not appear to be a way to rise above it or find any way out. So, no new idea could ever work, nobody could ever be trusted, everybody cheats and schemes to get ahead and to serve themselves, no fault can ever be overcome, no offense can ever be forgiven, everybody's against me, and the whole world is going to hell in a hand-basket.

Christian hope corrects chirpy optimism and overcomes cynical pessimism. Christian hope, as the Apostle Paul says, "does not disappoint us, because God's love has been poured into our hearts through the Holy Spirit which has been given to us" (Romans 5:5). He continues, "For in hope we were saved . . . [so] we know that all things work together for good for those who love God . . . " (Romans 8:24a, 28a). And as the Letter to the Hebrews chimes-in, "[Christian] hope is a sure and steadfast anchor for our souls" (6:19a).

God has placed the promise of God's hope before us, and since God is faithful to that promise, we can *trust* it!

The 9- and 10-year olds in Professor Migliore's story saw rainbows "way down low." Dorothy had looked "way up high," somewhere *over* the rainbow. But these east coast children had found hope not up in the sky, not way up high. Instead, they had found hope way down low in the grimy puddles of their city streets.

That's where *we* must look as well. We must look much lower. We must look around us. We must look within us. We must look to one another.

When God became human—when "the Word became flesh"—when the Incarnation arrived in little Bethlehem over 2000 years ago, Jesus did not appear in grandiose style in the sky "way up high." No, Jesus came on the scene just like every other baby, but his birthplace was in a barn, a stable, a manger that surely smelled of straw and manure, and mustiness and dinginess. Jesus came not as a king on a throne, but as a servant on a bed of hay.

And in this historical figure—and in the One who sent him—we place our hope. But this hope is not somewhere way up-high, *over* the rainbow. No, we find our hope way down-low, right here, right here in the shops and sidewalks and streets of our town, right here on this campus.

> Somewhere *under* the rainbow, way down *low*.
> There are hopes that we can cling
> to, a vision that we can know.
> Somewhere under the rainbow,
> hope is not actually blue,
> And the dreams that you dare to
> dream, really do come true.

Scripture for reflection: Genesis 9:8-17; Romans 5:1-5; 8:24-28; Hebrews 6:13-20

The Sweet Sorrow of Departure

> If you leave me now,
> you'll take away the biggest
> part of me; no, baby, please
> don't go.

These words from singer Peter Cetera may express in part some of the sentiments we feel today.

Although we bear the weight of pressure from papers, exams, meetings, reading assignments, exam preparation, exam grading, and end-of-the-year meetings, we know that very soon we will graduate our Senior Class.

College graduations have always been a bitter/sweet experience for me. On the one hand, they involve great joy and celebration . . . even relief: To know that you've made it, you've done it, you've accomplished it, *is* cause for rejoicing and festivity. Getting a college degree is no easy task—mentally, economically, psychologically, and temporally.

Mentally, there has been so much to learn. I was once given a t-shirt that read, "So many books, so little time." There *has* been so much to read, to master, to assimilate, to learn. And one of the things we learn in learning is *how* to learn. Learning skills in acquiring information, in organizing and analyzing information, and in applying information in practical ways is no less important than digesting and understanding specific information itself. There has been so much to learn.

Economically, it has not come cheaply! A long-time friend of mine, who has spent a lengthy time in higher education, once told me that a year of private college education could be likened to the purchase price of a mid-range family automobile. Through the years, that comparison has stood up: All students could have bought a nice car with the amount of money paid just this year to go to college. Your education has not come cheaply.

Psychologically, it also has not come without stress. A "stressor" is defined as "anything which produces stress." And stress may be understood as "the pressure to make adjustments in a relatively-brief period of time." So, if you have to work-in a research paper, an exam, a music recital, fraternity or sorority activities, Bible study preparation, and a part-time job into a tight temporal schedule, there is going to be stress. You and I know that there are inevitable and widely-felt moments in a semester which are "crazy times"—occasions when our psychological stability, even our sanity, is in jeopardy. You and I know those moments when we are "stressed out." Your education has not come without a psychological price.

Temporally, your education has not come without a price paid in time—one year, two years, three years, four years of commitment, dedication, and perseverance. You could've used the time in another way—joined the military and served a tour of duty; worked and saved money; gotten married and had some children; backpacked and hitchhiked around Europe. But you chose to spend your time in college. You've invested a significant chunk of time in higher education. Your education has not come without a temporal commitment—to use your time here doing what you've done, rather than using your time elsewhere doing something different.

Mentally, economically, psychologically, temporally—getting through a year of college, getting through four years of college and graduating have not been easy. Therefore, there need to be joy and celebration. There must be a moment to stop (before going on) to

A User-friendly Universe?

give thanks for what has been accomplished, to congratulate one's self, to congratulate others, and to be congratulated by others. There is a sweetness about graduation that excites us and satisfies us!

But I said that the end-of-the-year and graduation are bitter as well as sweet experiences. In the midst of the joy, underlying the celebration is a deep sense of sadness. Seniors will leave us; some students will choose (or be forced) not to return; some faculty or staff are moving on and will no longer be with us.

One of the earliest anxieties that a small child faces is what psychologists call "separation anxiety." A child is fearful that the one or ones on whom s/he depends will leave. I remember my own children, when they were little, grabbing my leg and holding-on for dear life! And if I would depart for another area of the house, they would run after me, for in the minds of children, not seeing me would mean that I had ceased to exist!

Good-bys from the side of those who remain are difficult, therefore, because we are both sad that valued persons will be leaving us and that we may not see them again. My Muslim friends always depart saying, "See you again, *ein shallah*" ('see you again, God-willing').

Goodbyes are also difficult from the side of those who are leaving. After relating to a certain group of persons with some degree of success, after knowing one's way around a given area, after coming to feel comfortable in a certain situation, after growing to cherish key individuals within that community, they leave.

It's anxiety-producing for those who are leaving, as well as for those who are staying behind. I know this place; I may be going to an unknown place. And even if I am returning to a place from which I originally came, that place will have changed while I was away. It was Thomas Wolfe who captured this insight when he stated, "A person can never go home." For home has changed since you were last there.

Surely Abraham must have felt this mishmash of sentiments, this bitter-sweetness of celebration and sadness, when he responded to God's call and departed familiar territory. Abraham is one of the Bible's earliest itinerants: He was mobile at a time when mass migrations of people were sweeping across the ancient Near Eastern portion of the world. And he came from a family that had already been on the move: His father, Terah, had moved from Ur in current-day Irag to Haran.

Abraham must have grown to enjoy Haran. He had lived there a long time; in fact, he was 75 years old when God told him it was time to move on! And yet, the promise of something new, something intended, something meaningful, was held out to him by God. Abraham had to overcome a fetish for the familiar with an openness to the future.

And so also do *we*: Our graduating Seniors will have to overcome a comfort with the known and cope with a discomfort with the unknown in order to be open to the future that God has in store for them. And those of us who stay here as a part of this institutional community will have to overcome a preference for things to remain the same and cope with an adjustment to a not-yet-known set of additions to our community next academic year in order to be open to the future that God has in store for us.

Abraham set out, not knowing exactly where he was going and what things would be like. But he did so, knowing that God would be with him every step of the way. And God *was* with Abraham: When Abraham came to the land of Canaan and went to the sacred tree of Moreh in the city of Shechem, the Lord appeared to him and reminded him that the promise, "I will give this land to your family forever," was still intact. And when Abraham left there to go to an area east of Bethel, he built an altar and worshipped the Lord.

We can expect nothing less; we can expect No One else. When the Israelites were perched on the edge of the "Red Sea" (*Yam suf*—"Sea of Reeds" or "Papyrus Lake"), the Lord said to Moses—

> Tell the Israelites to move forward. But lift up your staff, and stretch out your hand over the sea and

> divide it, that the Israelites may go into the sea on
> dry ground. (Exodus 14: 15b-16)

In other words, 'Move forward and the way will be provided.'

Those who are leaving our College can be encouraged with no other words—"Move forward and the way will be provided." Those of us who are remaining at our College can be encouraged with no less words—"Move forward as a community and the way will be provided."

But, in any case, "move forward." We can't live in the past, for that would stagnate us. We can't live as if the present will stay this way forever, for nothing in our temporal world defies change. So we can't cling either to the past or to the present, for that would distract us and stifle us. So, necessarily, we must move forward into the future.

The city of Colossae was an important location inland about 100 miles from the port city of Ephesus in what is contemporary Turkey. Paul had never been to Colossae and had not founded the church there; a man named Epaphras had done that. But Paul had heard about the strong faith of the Colossians.

As he learned more about the church there, Paul developed a grave concern about the Colossian Christians. Many, if not most, in the church at Colossae were Gentiles, and some of them were caught-up in a familiar and popular worship of angels and other spiritual powers believed to exist in the heavens between God and the world. Being so attached to, and distracted by, the influences of the culture around them, these Christians could not see that Christ is superior to every power and authority so that it was not necessary (nor even warranted) for Christians to worship them (Colossians 2:10, 20). Paul then tried to assure the Colossians that the forces of the universe didn't have any power over them and that they should not be duped by persons who brag about revelatory visions, but who in truth are spouting nonsense.

Paul wanted the Colossian Christians to get on with their discipleship, to move forward in their faith, to grow in their understanding of what their being in Christ means. If they belonged to Christ, they were *not* subject to any other power or authority. Since they were a part of Christ, they must not succumb to the temptations or influences around them, but must part company with all that and move forward.

We, too, must move forward. In order to avoid missing what God has in store for us, in order to grow and avoid stagnation, we must get on with it. As the old farmer said to the nervous young person leaving town for the first time and going off to college, "You can't get where you're going unless you leave where you are."

So, some of you will be leaving us: You *have* to, in order to get where you're going. This will be for us the "sweet sorrow of departure"—for we share your joy, but we are also sad. So, expect smiles and tears, expect good wishes and warm memories, expect our confused, contradictory, mixed-emotions of needing to let you go and wanting to hold-on to you.

> If you leave us now,
> you'll take away the biggest part of us;
> so that part of us wants to say,
> "Please don't go."
> But another part, a bigger, wiser
> part says, "Move forward, and the
> way will be provided. You can't
> get where you're going unless you
> leave where you are."

May God go with you (and with us).

Scripture for reflection: Genesis 12:1-9; Colossians 2:9-10, 18-23

About the Author

Clifford Chalmers Cain is the Harrod-C.S. Lewis Professor of Religious Studies and Chair of the Department at Westminster College in Fulton, Missouri. An ordained clergyperson and the holder of two doctorates, he has written seven previous books, many of them on the interface of religion and ecology and one of them at the intersection of theology and science.

Printed in the United States
By Bookmasters